Anne Orr's Classic Tatting Patterns

Dover Publications, Inc.
New York

Published in Canada by General Publishing Company, Ltd., 30 Lesmill Road, Don Mills, Toronto, Ontario.
Published in the United Kingdom by Constable and Company, Ltd., 10 Orange Street, London WC2H 7EG.

This Dover edition, first published in 1985, is an unabridged republication of *Tatting, Book No. 35, Revised*, as published by Anne Orr, Nashville, in 1940.

Manufactured in the United States of America
Dover Publications, Inc., 31 East 2nd Street, Mineola, N.Y. 11501

Library of Congress Cataloging in Publication Data

Orr, Anne Champe.
  Anne Orr's Classic tatting patterns.

  Reprint. Originally published: Tatting, book no. 35. Nashville : A. Orr, 1940.
  1. Tatting—Patterns. I. Title. III. Title: Classic tatting patterns.
TT840.077 1985   746.43′6041   85-4523
ISBN 0-486-24897-6

Centerpiece

Directions are on page 10

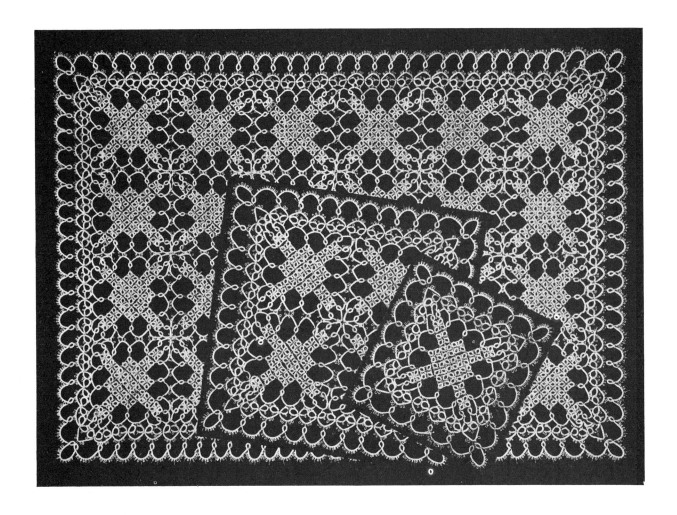

Rectangular Doily Set

(Use No. 40 Crochet Cotton and 2 Shuttles)

LARGE DOILY

Small Square Motif: R 3 ds, 3 p sep by 3 ds, 3 ds, cl, (r 3 ds, j in 3rd p of last r, 3 ds, 2 p sep by 3 ds, 3 ds, cl) twice, r 3 ds, j in 3rd p of last r, 3 ds, p, 3 ds, j in first p of first r, 3 ds, cl. Tie and cut.

Make 16 more small motifs and j together by center p of each motif as in illustration. Then, r 6 ds, j in right corner p of corner motif, 6 ds, cl, * ch 6 ds, 3 p sep by 2 ds, 6 ds, r 6 ds, j in next corner p of same motif, 6 ds, cl, ch 6 ds, 3 p sep by 2 ds, 6 ds, r 6 ds, j in p between 2 motifs, 6 ds, cl, ch 6 ds, 3 p sep by 2 ds, 6 ds, r 6 ds, j in p of next motif, 6 ds, cl, ch 6 ds, 3 p sep by 2 ds, 6 ds, r 6 ds, j in p between 2 motifs, 6 ds, cl, ch 6 ds, 3 p sep by 2 ds, 6 ds, r 6 ds, j in corner p of next motif, 6 ds, cl. Repeat from * around. Tie and cut.

Make 23 more motifs as above. Join each together as shown by center p of each ch.

1st row around: R 5 ds, j in first p of corner ch, 5 ds, 2 p sep by 5 ds, 5 ds, cl, ch 9 ds, 5 p sep by 2 ds, 9 ds, * r 5 ds, p, 5 ds, j in center p of last r, 5 ds, sk 1 p of ch, j in next p, 5 ds, cl, r 5 ds, j in first p of next ch, 5 ds. 2 p sep by 5 ds, 5 ds, cl, ch 6 ds, 5 p sep by 2 ds, 6 ds. Repeat from * around, making each corner as first was made.

2nd row: R 7 ds, j in center p of corner ch, 7 ds, cl, ch 5 ds, 12 p sep by 2 ds, 5 ds, r 7 ds, j in same p with last r, 7 ds, cl, * ch 5 ds, 9 p sep by 2 ds, 5 ds, r 7 ds, j in center p of next ch, 7 ds, cl. Repeat from * around, making each corner as first was made.

MEDIUM SIZE DOILY

Make 4 large motifs and j as for large doily. Then make 1st and 2nd rows like large doily.

SMALL DOILY

Make one large motif as for large doily. Then make 1st and 2nd rows around.

A Flower-Like Set

(Use No. 30 Crochet Cotton and 2 Shuttles)

LARGE DOILY

Center Ring: R 5 p sep by 2 ds, cl. Tie and cut.

1st row: * Sr 4 ds, p, 4 ds, cl, lr 4 ds, j to p of last r, 4 ds, j to p of center r, 4 ds, p, 4 ds, cl, sr 4 ds, j to last p of lr, 4 ds, cl. Ch (7 ds, p) twice, 7 ds. Repeat from * around center r. Tie and cut.

2nd row: Repeat first row. J each lr to a p of first row.

3rd row: Repeat 2nd row.

4th row: * Sr 4 ds, p, 4 ds, cl, lr 4 ds, j to p of sr, 4 ds, j to p of last row, 4 ds, p, 4 ds, cl, sr 4 ds, j to p of lr, 4 ds, cl, ch 7 ds, p, 7 ds. Repeat from * around. Tie and cut.

5th and 6th rows: Repeat 4th row.

7th row: * (Sr 4 ds, p, 4 ds, cl, lr 4 ds, j to p of sr, 4 ds, j to p of last row, 4 ds, p, 4 ds, cl, sr 4 ds, j to p of lr, 4 ds, cl, ch 7 ds, p, 7 ds) 4 times, sr 4 ds, p, 4 ds, cl, lr 4 ds, j to p of sr, 4 ds, j to p of last row, 4 ds, p, 4 ds, cl, sr 4 ds, j to p of lr, 4 ds, cl, ch (7 ds, p) twice, 7 ds. Repeat from * around. Tie and cut.

8th row: Repeat 2nd row.

9th row: Edge: Sr 4 ds, p, 4 ds, cl, lr 4 ds, j to p of sr, (4 ds, p) twice, 4 ds, cl, * sr 4 ds, j to p of lr, j to first p of a ch of last row, 4 ds, cl, sr 4 ds, j to next p of same ch of last row, p, 4 ds, cl, lr 4 ds, j to p of sr, (4 ds, p) twice, 4 ds, cl, sr 4 ds, j to p of lr, p, 4 ds, cl, (ch 4 ds, p, 4 ds, sr 4 ds, j to p of sr, p, 4 ds, cl, lr 4 ds, j to p of sr, 4 ds, p, 4 ds, p, 4 ds, cl, sr 4 ds, j to p of lr, p, 4 ds, cl) 3 times, (ch 4 ds, p, 4 ds, sr 4 ds, j to p of sr, p, 4 ds, cl, lr 4 ds, j to p of sr, 4 ds, j to center p of last lr, 4 ds, p 4 ds, cl, sr 4 ds, j to p of lr, p, 4 ds, cl) twice, (ch 4 ds, p, 4 ds, sr 4 ds, j to p of sr, p, 4 ds, cl, lr, 4 ds, j to p of sr, 4 ds, j to center p of opposite lr, 4 ds, p, 4 ds, cl, sr 4 ds, j to p of lr, p, 4 ds, cl) twice, ch 4 ds, p, 4 ds, sr 4 ds, j to p of sr, 4 ds, cl, lr 4 ds, j to p of sr, 4 ds, j to p of opposite lr, 4 ds, p, 4 ds, cl. Repeat from * around. Tie and cut.

MEDIUM DOILY

Make center ring, 1st, 2nd, 4th, 8th and 9th rows of large doily.

SMALL DOILY

Make center ring, 1st, 2nd and 9th rows.

Large Round Doily

(Use No. 60 Crochet Cotton and 2 Shuttles)

R 2 ds, 5 p with 3 ds between, cl, tie and cut.

1st row: R 2 ds, p, 2 ds, j to a p of center r, 2 ds, p, 2 ds, cl, * ch 2 ds, 5 p sep by 2 ds, 2 ds, r 2 ds, p, 2 ds, j to next p of center r, 2 ds, p, 2 ds, cl, repeat from * around. Tie and cut.

2nd row: R 2 ds, p, 2 ds, j to second p of ch (counting from left), 2 ds, p, 2 ds, cl, * ch 10 ds, r 2 ds, p, 2 ds, sk 1 p on ch, j to next p, 2 ds, p, 2 ds, cl, repeat from * around, j r to second and fourth p on p ch of last row, j to first r.

3rd row: Ch 2 ds, 5 p sep by 2 ds, 2 ds, j between preceding row. Repeat around. Tie and cut.

4th row: R 2 ds, p, 2 ds, j in second p of ch, 2 ds, p, 2 ds, cl, * ch 2 ds, 5 p sep by 2 ds, 2 ds, r 2 ds, p, 2 ds, j to fourth p of same ch, 2 ds, p, 2 ds, cl, repeat from *, j r to second and fourth p on p ch of last row, tie and cut.

5th row: * R 10 ds, j to center p on ch, 10 ds, cl, ch 10 ds, repeat from * around.

6th row: * Ch 2 ds, 5 p sep by 2 ds, 2 ds, j between ch of preceding row. Tie and cut.

7th row: R 2 ds, 5 p sep by 2 ds, 2 ds, cl, r 2 ds, j to fifth p of last r, 2 ds, p, 2 ds, j to center p of ch (last row), 2 ds, p, 2 ds, p, 2 ds, cl, * r 2 ds, j to fifth p of last r, 2 ds, 4 p sep by 2 ds, 2 ds, cl, ch 2 ds, 10 p sep by 2 ds, 2 ds, r 2 ds, p, 2 ds, p, 2 ds, cl, r 2 ds, j to fifth p of last r, 2 ds, p, 2 ds, j to center p of next ch, 2 ds. p, 2 ds, p, 2 ds, cl, repeat from * around. Tie and cut.

Continued on Page 29

A Simple Set

(Use No. 10 Crochet Cotton and 2 Shuttles)

R 4 ds, p, 3 ds, p, 3 ds, p, 4 ds, cl; r 4 ds, j to last p of 1st r, 2 ds, 4 p sep by 2 ds, 4 ds, cl; r 4 ds, j to last p of 2nd r, 3 ds, p, 3 ds, p, 4 ds, cl. Ch 8 ds, turn, r 4 ds, p, 3 ds, j to last p of last r of first cluster, 3 ds, p, 4 ds, cl.

* R 4 ds, j to last p of last r, 2 ds, 4 p sep by 2 ds, 4 ds, cl, r 4 ds, j to last p of 2nd r, 3 ds, p, 3 ds, p, 4 ds, cl. Turn, ch 7 ds, 3 p sep by 2 ds, 7 ds, turn, r 4 ds, p, 3 ds, j to center p of last r, 3 ds, p, 4 ds, cl. Repeat from * until desired length is reached, about 18 inches for place mat and 26 inches for runner.

Ch 8 ds, r 4 ds, j to 2nd p of last r in last cluster, 3 ds, p, 3 ds, p, 4 ds, cl, r 4 ds, j to last p in first r, 2 ds, 4 p sep by 2 ds, 4 ds, cl.

R 4 ds, j to last p of 2nd r, 3 ds, p, 3 ds, p, 4 ds, cl, turn. Ch 8 ds, turn, r 4 ds, p, 3 ds, j to last p of 3rd r of last cluster. * Finish cluster with 2 r, turn, ch 7 ds, j to last p in ch as shown, 2 ds, j to 2nd p, 2 ds, j to 3rd p, 7 ds, turn, r 4 ds, p, 3 ds, j to 2nd p of last r in last cluster. Repeat from *.

To finish off j 2nd p of 3rd r of last cluster to 1st p of 1st cluster, turn, ch 8 ds, fasten off.

For a place mat, make 9 finished strips, j by the center p of last r as the work proceeds. For the runner make 9 strips of 36 clusters each.

A Lacy Set

(Use No. 30 Crochet Cotton and 2 Shuttles)

LARGE DOILY

For Motifs: R 3 ds, 3 p sep by 3 ds, 3 ds, cl, (r 3 ds, j in last p of last r, 3 ds, 2 p sep by 3 ds, 3 ds, cl) twice, r 3 ds, j in last p of last r, 3 ds, p, 3 ds, j in p of first r, 3 ds, cl. Tie and cut. Make 4 more small motifs, j at corners as in illustration.

Then, r 6 ds, j in center p of r of last row, 6 ds, cl, * ch 9 ds, p, 3 ds, r 3 ds, p, 3 ds, cl, ch 3 ds, p, 9 ds, r 6 ds, j in center p of next r of last row, 6 ds, cl. Repeat from * around. Tie and cut.

Make 3 more motifs as one just made. Join together by p of small r of last row as in illustration to form a diamond.

1st row around: R 3 ds, j in p of first small r to left on side where 2 motifs were j, 3 ds, cl, * r 3 ds, j in p of first sr of next motif, 3 ds, cl, (ch 4 ds, 9 p sep by 2 ds, 4 ds, r 3 ds, j in p of next sr of same motif, 3 ds, cl, r 3 ds, j in same p with last r, 3 ds, cl) 3 times, ch 4 ds, 9 p sep by 2 ds, 4 ds, r 3 ds, j in p of next sr, 3 ds, cl, r 3 ds, j in p of sr of next motif, 3 ds, cl, (ch 4 ds, 9 p sep by 2 ds, 4 ds, r 3 ds, j in p of next sr, 3 ds, cl, r 3 ds, j in same p with last r, 3 ds, cl) twice, ch 6 ds, 12 p sep by 2 ds,

6 ds, (r 3 ds, j in p of next sr, 3 ds, cl, r 3 ds, j in same p with last r, 3 ds, cl, ch 4 ds, 9 p sep by 2 ds, 4 ds) twice, r 3 ds, j in p of next sr, 3 ds, cl. Repeat from * around. Tie and cut.

2nd row: R 2 ds, 4 p, j in 2nd p to right of end ch of 12 p of last row, 4 p, 2 ds, cl, (ch 6 ds, 3 p sep by 2 ds, 6 ds, r 2 ds, 4 p, sk 2 p, j in next p, 4 p, 2 ds, cl) 3 times, * ch 6 ds, 3 p sep by 2 ds, 6 ds, r 2 ds, 4 p, sk 1 p of next ch, j in next p, 4 p, 2 ds, cl, (ch 6 ds, 3 p sep by 2 ds, 6 ds, r 2 ds, 4 p, sk 2 p of same ch, j in next p, 4 p, 2 ds, cl) twice. Repeat from * around, tie and cut.

3rd row: * R 5 ds, j in center p of ch of last row, 5 ds, cl, ch 6 ds, 3 p sep by 2 ds, 6 ds, repeat around from *, tie and cut.

4th row: * R 2 ds, 4 p, j in center p of ch of last row, 4 p, 2 ds, cl, ch 7 ds, 3 p sep by 2 ds, 7 ds. Repeat from * around, making 3 chs at each end as follows: Ch 8 ds, 3 p sep by 2 ds, 8 ds, tie and cut.

5th row: * R 5 ds, j in center p of ch of last row, 5 ds,

Continued on Page 10

—8—

Rectangular Luncheon Set

LARGE DOILY

(Use No. 30 Crochet Cotton, and 2 Shuttles)

Center Small Motifs: (R 6 ds, 3 p sep by 4 ds, 6 ds, cl) 4 times. Tie and cut.

Make two rows of the motifs with five motifs each. Join together by side p, leaving center p of r free.

1st row: *R 6 ds, p, 5 ds, j to center p of r of corner motif, 5 ds, p, 6 ds, cl, turn, ch 5 ds, 7 p sep by 2 ds, 5 ds, turn, r 6 ds, p, 5 ds, j to same p with last r, 5 ds p, 6 ds, cl (turn, ch 5 ds, 5 p sep by 2 ds, 5 ds, turn, r 6 ds, j to center p of next r, 5 ds, j to center p of next r, 6 ds, cl) 4 times, turn, ch 5 ds, 5 p sep by 2 ds, 5 ds, turn, r 6 ds, p, 5 ds, j to center p of next r, 5 ds, p, 6 ds, cl, turn, ch 5 ds, 7 p sep by 2 ds, 5 ds, turn, r 6 ds, p, 5 ds, j to same p with last r, 5 ds, p, 6 ds, cl, turn, ch 5 ds, 5 p sep by 2 ds, 5 ds, turn, r 6 ds, j to center p of next r, 5 ds, j to center p of next r, 6 ds, cl, turn, ch 5 ds, 5 p sep by 2 ds, 5 ds, turn. Repeat from * around. Tie and cut.

2d row: Lr 3 ds, 6 p sep by 3 ds, 3 ds, cl, turn, ch 3 ds, 7 p sep by 2 ds, 3 ds, turn, r 5 ds, j to sixth p of lr, 5 ds, cl, turn, ch 4 ds, turn, r 5 ds, j to fifth p of lr, 5 ds, cl, turn, ch 4 ds, turn, r 5 ds, p, 5 ds, cl, r 5 ds, j to p of last r, 5 ds, j to third p of corner ch (last row), 5 ds, p, 5 ds, cl, r 5 ds, j to third p of last r, 5 ds, cl (turn, ch 4 ds, turn, r 5 ds, p, 5 ds, cl) twice, j to ch on opposite side, turn, ch 3 ds

7 p sep by 2 ds, 3 ds, turn, lr 3 ds, j to p of last r, 3 ds, j to p of next r, 3 ds, 4 p sep by 3 ds, 3 ds, cl, turn, ch 3 ds, 7 p sep by 2 ds, 3 ds, turn, r 5 ds, j to sixth p of lr, 5 ds, cl, turn, ch 4 ds, turn, r 5 ds, j to fifth p of lr, 5 ds, cl, turn, ch 4 ds, turn, r 5 ds, p, 5 ds, cl, r 5 ds, j to p of last r, 5 ds, sk 1 p on same corner ch, j to next p, 5 ds, p, 5 ds, cl, r 5 ds j to third p of last r, 5 ds, cl, * (turn, ch 4 ds, turn, r 5 ds, p, 5 ds, cl) twice, j to ch on opposite side, turn, ch 3 ds, 7 p sep by 2 ds, 3 ds, turn, lr 3 ds, j to p of last r, 3 ds, j to p of next r, 3 ds, 4 p sep by 3 ds, 3 ds, cl, turn, ch 3 ds, 7 p sep by 2 ds, 3 ds, turn, r 5 ds, j to sixth p of lr, 5 ds, cl, turn, ch 4 ds, turn, r 5 ds, j to fifth p of lr, 5 ds, cl, turn, ch 4 ds, turn, r 5 ds, p, 5 ds, cl, r 5 ds, j to p of last r, 5 ds, j to center p of next ch (last row), 5 ds, p, 5 ds, cl, r 5 ds, j to third p of last r, 5 ds, cl. Repeat from * around. When corners are reached, repeat like first corner. Tie and cut.

Make four small motifs of three r each for corners as follows: R 3 ds, p, 3 ds, j to center p of ch in corner, 3 ds, 3 p sep by 3 ds, 3 ds, cl, r 3 ds, j to fifth p of last r, 3 ds, 4 p sep by 3 ds, 3 ds, cl, r 3 ds, j to fifth p of last r, 3 ds, 2 p sep by 3 ds, 3 ds, j to center p of next ch in the corner 3 ds, p, 3 ds, cl. Tie and cut.

3d row: R 6 ds, j to second p of center r of small motif, 6 ds, cl, turn, ch 6 ds, 3 p sep by 2 ds, 6 ds, turn, r 6 ds, j to fourth p of same r, 6 ds, cl, turn, ch 6 ds, 3 p sep by 2 ds, 6 ds, turn, r 6 ds, j to second p of next r, 6 ds, cl, *

Continued on Page 18

Elaborate Luncheon Set

(On Page 32)

(Use No. 50 Crochet Cotton and 2 Shuttles)

Round Motif: 1st Row: R 7 ds, L p, 7 ds, cl, (ch 10 ds, r 7 ds, j to L p, 7 ds, cl) 5 times, ch 10 ds. Tie and cut (6 rings).

2nd row: J cotton between 2 ch of last row, * (ch 5 ds, p) twice, 5 ds, j between next 2 ch of last row. Repeat from * around. Tie and cut.

3rd row: R 7 ds, j to p of last row, 7 ds, cl, * ch 10 ds, r 7 ds, j to next p of last row, 7 ds, cl. Repeat from * around. Tie and cut.

4th row: J cotton between 2 ch of last row, * ch 3 ds, 5 p sep by 2 ds, 3 ds, j between next 2 ch of last row. Repeat from * around. Tie and cut.

Leaf Motif: R 3 ds, 3 p sep by 2 ds, 3 ds, cl, ch 7 ds, p, 2 ds, r 6 ds, j to last p of last r, 2 ds, 3 p sep by 2 ds, 6 ds, cl, ch 7 ds, p, 2 ds, r 8 ds, j to last p of last r, 2 ds, 3 p sep by 2 ds, 8 ds, cl, ch 7 ds, p, 2 ds, r 6 ds, j to last p of last r, 2 ds, 3 p sep by 2 ds, 6 ds, cl, ch 7 ds, j, 2 ds, p, 7 ds, p, 7 ds, r 6 ds, sk 1 p of last ch, j in next p, 4 ds, j in last p of last r, 3 ds, p, 4 ds, cl, ch 2 ds, p, 7 ds, r 6 ds, j in p of last r, 1 ds, j in next p of opposite r, 2 ds, j in next p of same r, 2 ds, p, 6 ds, cl, ch 2 ds, p, 7 ds, r 8 ds, j to p of last r, 2 ds, j to p of opposite r, 2 ds, j to next p of same r, 2 ds, p, 8 ds, cl, ch 2 ds, p, 7 ds, r 6 ds, j to p of last r, 2 ds, j to next p of opposite r, 2 ds, j to next p of same r, 2 ds, p, 6 ds, cl, ch 2 ds, p, 7 ds, r 3 ds, j to p of last r, 2 ds, j to p of opposite r, 2 ds, j to next p of same r, 3 ds, cl, ch 2 ds, p, 7 ds, j in center p of ch of round motif, j in p with last r, 7 ds, p, 2 ds, j to first r. Tie and cut. Make 12 leaves as above. Join 1 to each ch of motif. Join the leaves together in groups of 2 by 2 p. The longer leaves are made in same way by adding 3 rings with 6 ds and 2

with 8 ds, on each side of leaf. Join motifs together as shown in illustration.

The center motif for tumbler doily has 5 rings in center instead of 6 rings as for other round motifs. Join all motifs as in illustration, then make stems.

STEMS: Join cotton to center p of center ch of round motif with 8 leaves around. Ch 10 ds, p, 20 ds, p, 15 ds, p, 12 ds, j to center p of ch of opposite round motif. Tie and cut.

Join cotton to center of base of 2nd leaf, ch 5 ds, j to last p of long stem, 5 ds, j to center at base of opposite leaf. Tie and cut.

Join cotton to center of base of 3rd leaf, ch 6 ds, j to next p of long stem, 6 ds, j to center of base of opposite leaf. Tie and cut.

Join cotton to center of base of 4th leaf, ch 7 ds, j to next p of long stem, 7 ds, j to center of base of opposite leaf. Tie and cut.

TUMBLER DOILY

Has center made with 5 rings and 10 leaves around. Around this, place 12 round motifs.

PLATE DOILY

Center has 6 rings with 12 leaves around. Around this, put 6 round motifs alternated with 6 long leaves. Then on outside make 18 round motifs.

CENTERPIECE (On Page 3)

Make plate doily. Around this put 6 tumbler doilies and between this make the stem and leaves as shown.

A LACY SET

Continued from Page 8

cl, ch 8 ds, p, 2 ds, r 3 ds, p, 3 ds, cl, ch 2 ds, p, 8 ds, repeat from * around, tie and cut.

6th row: * R 14 ds, j in p of sr of last row, 14 ds, cl, ch 8 ds, 5 p sep by 2 ds, 8 ds, repeat from * around, tie and cut.

7th row: * R 2 ds, 4 p, j in center p of ch of last row, 4 p, 2 ds, cl, ch 8 ds, 5 p sep by 2 ds, 8 ds, repeat from * around, tie and cut.

8th row: R 3 ds, 3 p sep by 3 ds, 3 ds, cl, (r 3 ds, j in last p of last r, 3 ds, 2 p sep by 3 ds, 3 ds, cl) twice, r 3 ds, j in last p of last r, 3 ds, j in center p of ch of last row, 3 ds, j in first p of first r, 3 ds, cl. Tie and cut. R 3 ds, 3 p sep by 3 ds, 3 ds, cl. R 3 ds, j to last p of last r, 3 ds, 2 sep by 3 ds, 3 ds, cl, r 3 ds, j to last p of last r, 3 ds, j in p of r of last small motif, 3 ds, p 3 ds, cl, r 3 ds, j in p of last r, 3 ds, j in center p of next ch of last row, 3 ds, j in p of first r, 3 ds, cl. Tie and cut. R 3 ds, 3 p sep by 3 ds, 3 ds, cl, r 3 ds, j in last p of last r, 3 ds, 2 p sep by 3 ds, 3 ds, cl. R 3 ds, j in p of last r, 3 ds, j in p of r of last

motif, 3 ds, p, 3 ds, cl. R 3 ds, j in p of last r, 3 ds, sk 1 p of next ch, j in next p, 3 ds, j in p of first r, 3 ds, cl. Tie and cut. R 3 ds, 3 p sep by 3 ds, 3 ds, cl, r 3 ds, j in last p of last r, 3 ds, 2 p sep by 3 ds, 3 ds, cl. R 3 ds, j in p of last r, 3 ds, j in p of r of last motif, 3 ds, p, 3 ds, cl. R 3 ds, j in p of last r, 3 ds, sk 1 p of same ch, j in next p, 3 ds, j in p of first r. Tie and cut. Repeat these four motifs halfway around doily ending as first 2 motifs were joined, then be sure to j 2 more as first 2 were j and repeat as first half was made. When this is finished, make the small motifs and j between every other one as in illustration.

9th row: R 5 ds, j in p of motif in last row, 5 ds, cl, * r 5 ds, j in same p with last r, 5 ds, cl, ch 7 ds, 12 p sep by 2 ds, 7 ds, r 5 ds, j in p of next motif of last row, 5 ds, cl. Repeat from * around. Tie and cut.

SMALL DOILY

Make the 4 motifs and first row as for large doily.

Oval Doily Set

MEDALLION

(Use No. 30 Thread and 2 Shuttles)

1st row: R 5 ds, 3 p sep by 5 ds, 5 ds, cl, (ch 7 ds, p, 7 ds, r 5 ds, j to third p of last r, 5 ds, 2 p sep by 5 ds, 5 ds, cl) 7 times, j eighth r to first r, ch 7 ds, p, 7 ds. Tie and cut.

2nd row: R 5 ds, p, 5 ds, j to p of ch of last row, 5 ds, p, 5 ds, cl, * ch 7 ds, p, 7 ds, r 5 ds, j to third p of last r, 5 ds, 2 p sep by 5 ds, 5 ds, cl, ch 7 ds, p, 7 ds, r 5 ds, j to third p of last r, 5 ds, j to p of next ch of last row. 5 ds, p, 5 ds, cl. Repeat from * around. Tie and cut.

3rd row: R 9 ds, lp, 9 ds, cl, ch 7 ds, 2 p sep by 2 ds, 2 ds, j to p of ch of last row, 2 ds, 2 p sep by 2 ds, 7 ds, r 9 ds, lp, 9 ds, cl, (ch 7 ds, 5 p sep by 2 ds, 7 ds, r 9 ds, j to lp of last r, 9 ds, cl) 3 times, * ch 7 ds, 2 p sep by 2 ds, sk 1 ch of last row, j to p of next ch, 2 ds, 2 p sep by 2 ds, 7 ds, r 9 ds, lp, 9 ds, cl, ch 7 ds, p, 2 ds, j to fourth p of opposite ch, 2 ds, 3 p sep by 2 ds, 7 ds, (r 9 ds, j to lp of last r, 9 ds, cl, ch 7 ds, 5 p sep by 2 ds, 7 ds) twice, r 9 ds, j to same lp, 9 ds, cl. Repeat from * around. Tie and cut.

Make 3 medallions and j together by center p of 2 ch as in illustration. Make a short row between each 2 medallions on either side as follows: Sr 6 ds, p, 6 ds, cl, ch 6 ds, 2 p sep by 2 ds, 2 ds, j to third p of second ch from where the 2 medallions are j, 2 ds, 2 p sep by 2 ds, 6 ds, lr 5

ds, j to p of sr, 2 ds, 10 p sep by 2 ds, 5 ds, cl, ch 6 ds, 5 p sep by 2 ds, 6 ds, sr 6 ds, j to last p of lr, 6 ds, cl, sr 6 ds, p, 6 ds, cl, ch 6 ds, 5 p sep by 2 ds, 6 ds, lr 5 ds, j to p of sr, 2 ds, 10 p sep by 2 ds, 5 ds, cl, ch 6 ds, 2 p sep by 2 ds, 2 ds, j to third p of second ch from where the 2 medallions j, 2 ds, 2 p sep by 2 ds, 6 ds, sr 6 ds, j to last p of lr, 6 ds, cl. Tie and cut.

1st row around the 3 medallions of center: Lr 5 ds, 5 p sep by 2 ds, 2 ds, j to center p of first ch of end medallion, to right of the short row, 2 ds, 5 p sep by 2 ds, 5 ds, cl, (ch 6 ds, 5 p sep by 2 ds, 6 ds, sr 6 ds, j to last p of lr, 6 ds, cl, sr 6 ds, p, 6 ds, cl, ch 6 ds, 5 p sep by 2 ds, 6 ds, lr 5 ds, j to p of sr, 2 ds, 10 p sep by 2 ds, 5 ds, cl, ch 6 ds, 5 p sep by 2 ds, 6 ds, sr 6 ds, j to last p of lr, 6 ds, cl, sr 6 ds, p, 6 ds, cl, ch 6 ds, 5 p sep by 2 ds, 6 ds, lr 5 ds, j to p of sr, 2 ds, 4 p sep by 2 ds, 2 ds, j to center p of next ch of medallion, 2 ds, 5 p sep by 2 ds, 5 ds, cl) 5 times, (ch 6 ds, 5 p sep by 2 ds, 6 ds, sr 6 ds, j to last p of lr, 6 ds, cl, sr 6 ds, p, 6 ds, cl, ch 6 ds, 5 p sep by 2 ds, 6 ds, lr 5 ds, j to p of sr, 2 ds, 4 p sep by 2 ds, 2 ds, j to center p of lr of short row, 2 ds, 5 p sep by 2 ds, 5 ds, cl) twice, ch 6 ds, 5 p sep by 2 ds, 6 ds, sr 6 ds, j to last p of lr, 6 ds, cl, sr 6 ds, p, 6 ds, cl, ch 6 ds, 5 p sep by 2 ds, 6 ds, lr 5 ds, j to p of sr, 2 ds, 4 p sep by 2 ds, 2 ds, j to center p of ch of next medallion, 2 ds, 5 p sep by 2 ds, 5 ds, cl, ch

Continued on Page 27

Directions for Medallions

SIXTEEN POINTED MEDALLION (1st Column, Top)
(2 Shuttles)

1st row: (R 4 ds, p, 4 ds, cl, turn, ch 10 ds, turn) 8 times. Tie and cut.

2d row: *(R 4 ds, j to p of r (last row) 4 ds, cl) twice. turn, ch 3 ds, 4 p sep by 2 ds, 3 ds, turn, repeat from * around. Tie and cut.

3d row: *R 4 ds, p, 4 ds, cl, turn, ch 7 ds, j to first p of ch, ch, 7 ds, turn, r 4 ds, p, 4 ds, cl, turn, ch 7 ds, sk 2 p of same ch, j in next p, ch 7 ds, turn, repeat from * around. Tie and cut.

MEDALLION (1st Column, Center)
(2 Shuttles)

1st row: R 4 ds, 3 p sep by 4 ds, 4 ds, cl, (sp ⅛-inch, r 4 ds, j to third p of last r, 4 ds, 2 p sep by 4 ds, 4 ds, cl) 9 times, j last r to first r. Tie and cut.

2d row: *R 8 ds, p, 8 ds, cl, ch 8 ds, j to p of last row, 8 ds. Repeat from * around. Tie and cut.

3d row: *R 3 ds, j to p of r of last row, 4 ds, lp, 7 ds, cl, ch 9 ds, p, 9 ds, j to lp of last r, r 7 ds, lp, 7 ds, cl, ch 9 ds, p, 9s, j to lp of last r. Repeat from * around. Tie and cut.

SUNFLOWER MEDALLION (1st Column, Bottom)
(2 Shuttles)

R 11 lp, cl. Tie and cut.

1st row: Lr 5 ds, p, 5 ds, p, 6 ds, p, 6 ds, p, 5 ds, p, 5 ds, cl, * j to p of center r, r 5 ds, j to fifth p of last r, 5 ds, j to fourth p of last r, 6 ds, p, 6 ds, 2 p sep by 5 ds, 5 ds, cl. Repeat from * around. Tie and cut.

2d row: *R 4 ds, p, 4 ds, cl, j to p of lr, (last row), turn, ch 12 ds, turn. Repeat from * around. Tie and cut.

3d row: *(R 4 ds, j to p of r (last row), 4 ds, cl) twice, turn, ch 7 ds, p, 7 ds, turn. Repeat from * around. Tie and cut.

LARGE ROUND MEDALLION WITH CROSS IN CENTER (2d Column, Top)
(2 Shuttles)

Small motifs for center: R 6 ds, p, 3 ds, 3 p sep by 2 ds, 3 ds, p, 6 ds, cl, (r 6 ds, j to fifth p of last r, 3 ds, 3 p sep by 2 ds, 3 ds, p, 6 ds, cl) 3 times, j last r to first r. Tie and cut.

Make 4 more small motifs like first one. Join one to center p of each r of first motif.

1st row: R 5 ds, 3 p sep by 5 ds, 5 ds, cl, * turn, ch 8 ds, p, 8 ds, turn, r 5 ds, j to third p of last r, 5 ds, j to center p of motif, 5 ds, p, 5 ds, cl, (turn, ch 8 ds, p, 8 ds, turn, r 5 ds, j to third p of last r, 5 ds, 2 p sep by 5 ds, 5 ds, cl) 5 times. Repeat from * around. Tie and cut.

2d row: *R 9 ds, j to p of ch (last row), 9 ds cl, turn, ch 8 ds, turn, (r 9 ds, p, 9 ds, cl) three times, turn, ch 9 ds. Repeat from * around. Tie and cut.

MEDALLION (2d Column, Center)
(2 Shuttles)

1st row: *(R 4 ds, p, 4 ds, cl) twice, j second r to first by p, turn, ch 4 ds, 3 p sep by 2 ds, 4 ds, turn. Repeat from * until there are 6 groups of 2 r, and 6 ch. Tie and cut.

2d row: *R 4 ds, p, 4 ds, cl, turn, ch 8 ds, j to first p of ch (last row), r 4 ds, p, 4 ds, cl, turn, ch 8 ds, j to third p of ch (last row), r 4 ds, p, 4 ds, cl, turn, ch 8 ds, turn, repeat from * around. Tie and cut.

3d row: *R 4 ds, j to p of r over group of 2 r of first row, 4 ds, cl, turn, ch 9 ds, p, 9 ds, turn, r 4 ds, j to next

p of r (last row), 4 ds, cl, r 4 ds, p, 4 ds, cl, r 4 ds, j to p of next r (last row), 4 ds, cl, turn, ch 9 ds, p, 9 ds, turn. Repeat from * around. Tie and cut.

SQUARE MEDALLION (2d Column, Bottom)
(2 Shuttles)

For Center: Make four small motifs as follows: R 4 ds, 7 p, 4 ds, cl, (r 4 ds, j to seventh p of last r, 6 p, 4 ds, cl) three times. Join last r to first r. Tie and cut. Join motifs by center p of 2 r to form a square. Then make four motifs with 3 r each and j first and third r to second and sixth p of corner r

Last row: *R 4 ds, 4 p, j to p between two motifs, 4 p, 4 ds, cl, turn, ch 3 ds, 5 p, 3 ds, j to fifth p of next r, ch 3 ds, 5 p, 3 ds, j to center p of corner r, ch 3 ds, 5 p, 3 ds, j to third p of next r, ch 3 ds, 5 p, 3 ds, turn. Repeat from * around. Tie and cut.

ROUND MEDALLION (3d Column, Top)
(2 Shuttles)

Center: R 7 ds, 3 p sep by 7 ds, 7 ds, cl, (r 7 ds, j to third p of last r, 7 ds, 2 p sep by 7 ds, 7 ds, cl,) three times. Join last r to first r. Tie and cut.

1st row: R 5 ds, p, 4 ds, *j to p between 2 lr (center) 4 ds, p, 5 ds, cl, turn, ch 3 ds, 4 p sep by 2 ds, 3 ds, turn, r 4 ds, j to third p of last r, 4 ds j to center p of lr, 4 ds, p, 5 ds, cl, turn, ch 3 ds, 4 p sep by 2 ds, 3 ds, turn, r 5 ds, j to third p of last r, 4 ds, j to same p with last r, 4 ds, p, 5 ds, cl, turn, ch 3 ds, 4 p sep by 2 ds, 3 ds, turn, r 5 ds, j to third p of last r, 4 ds, repeat from * around. Tie and cut.

2d row: Lr 4 ds, 3 p sep by 4 ds, 4 ds, cl, *turn, ch 4 ds, turn, sr 4 ds, j to first p of ch (last row) 4 ds, cl, turn, ch 4 ds, turn, lr 4 ds, j to third p of last lr, 4 ds, 2 p sep by 4 ds, 4 ds, cl, turn, ch 4 ds, turn, sr 4 ds, j to fourth p of same ch, 4 ds, cl, turn, ch 4 ds, turn, lr 4 ds, j to third p of last lr, 4 ds, 2 p sep by 4 ds, 4 ds, cl, repeat from * around. Tie and cut.

MEDALLION (3d Column, Center)
(2 Shuttles)

1st row: R 3 ds, 3 p sep by 3 ds, 3 ds, cl, (sp ⅛-inch, r 3 ds, j to third p of last r, 3 ds, 2 p sep by 3 ds, 3 ds, cl) five times, j last r to first r, (6 in all). Tie and cut.

2d row: *R 3 ds, p, 3 ds, j to p of r of last row, 3 ds, p, 3 ds, cl, ch 6 ds, 3 p sep by 6 ds, 6 ds. Repeat from * around. Tie and cut.

3d row: R 3 ds, 3 p sep by 3 ds, 3 ds, cl, * ch 8 ds, 4 p sep by 8 ds, 3 ds, r 3 ds, p, 3 ds, j to third p of last r, 3 ds, p, 3 ds, cl, ch 3 ds, r 3 ds, p, 3 ds, j to center p of ch of last row, 3 ds, p, 3 ds, cl, ch 3 ds, r 3 ds, 3 p sep by 3 ds, 3 ds, cl, ch 3 ds, j to p of last ch, 8 ds, 3 p sep by 8 ds, 8 ds, r 3 ds, j to center p of last r, 3 ds, 2 p sep by 3 ds, 3 ds, cl. Repeat from * around. Tie and cut.

ROUND MEDALLION (3d Column, Bottom)
(2 Shuttles)

Center: R 2 ds, 4 lp sep by 3 ds, cl. Tie and cut.

1st row: R 8 ds, j to lp of center, 8 ds, cl, * turn, ch 4 ds, 3 p sep by 3 ds, 4 ds, turn, r 8 ds, j to same lp with last r, 8 ds, cl, turn, ch 4 ds, 3 p sep by 3 ds, 4 ds, turn, r 8 ds, j to next lp 8 ds, cl. Repeat from * around. Tie and cut.

2d row: R 8 ds, p, 8 ds, cl, * r 8 ds, j to center p of ch (last row), 8 ds, cl, r 8 ds, p, 8 ds, cl, turn, ch 6 ds, p, 6 ds, turn, r 4 ds, j to p of last r, 4 ds, 2 p sep by 4 ds, 4 ds, cl, turn, ch 6 ds, p, 6 ds, turn, r 8 ds, j to third p of last r, 8 ds, cl. Repeat from * around. Tie and cut.

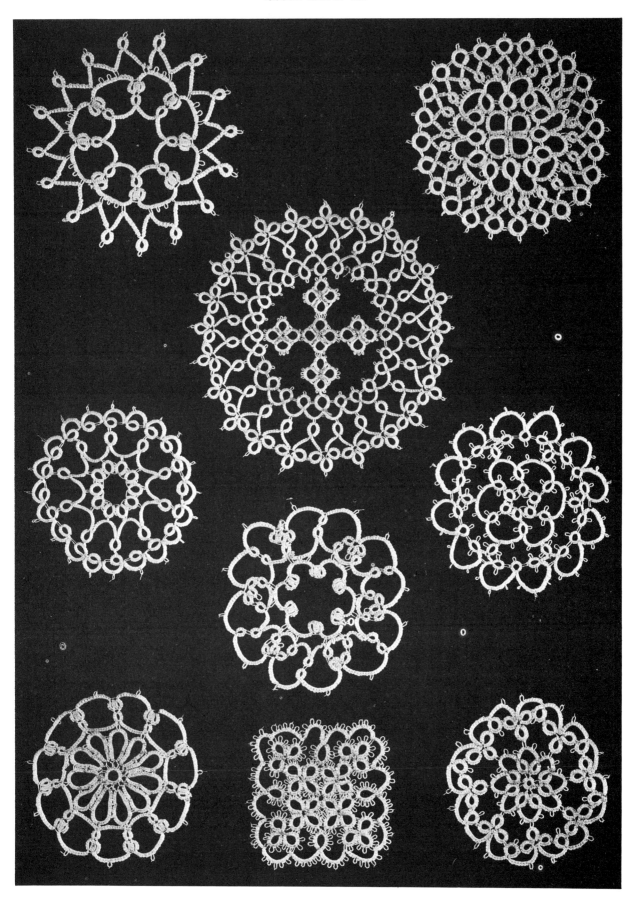

Directions for Medallions

ROUND MEDALLION (Top Row, Left)
(2 Shuttles)

Center: R 6 ds, p, 6 ds, p, 3 ds, p, 3 ds, p, 6 ds, p, 6 ds, cl, repeat r 3 times, j first p to last p of last r, j last p of last r to first p of first r. Tie and cut.

1st row: R 4 ds, p, 4 ds, j to first free p of center, 4 ds, p, 4 ds, cl, * ch 6 ds, p, 6 ds, r 4 ds, j to last p of last r, 4 ds, j to next p of center, 4 ds, p, 4 ds, cl. Repeat from * all around. Tie and cut.

2d row: R 4 ds, p, 4 ds, j to p of ch of first row, 4 ds, p, 4 ds, cl, * ch 6 ds, p, 6 ds, r 4 ds, j to p of last r, 4 ds, p, 4 ds, cl, ch 6 ds, p, 6 ds, r 4 ds, j to p of last r, 4 ds, j to p of next ch of first row, 4 ds, p, 4 ds, cl. Repeat from * all around. Tie and cut.

SQUARE MEDALLION (Top Row, Center)
(2 Shuttles)

1st row: R 5 ds, p, 8 ds, p, 5 ds, cl, (turn, ch 6 ds, p, 3 ds, p, 6 ds, turn, r 5 ds, j to second p of last r, 8 ds, p, 5 ds, cl) 7 times, turn, ch 6 ds, p, 3 ds, p, 6 ds. Tie and cut.

2d row: Lr 12 ds, p, 12 ds, cl, turn, ch 4 ds, p, *14 ds, p, 4 ds, j in p of lr, turn, r 4 ds, j to p of ch, 5 ds, 2 p sep by 5 ds, 4 ds, cl, (r 4 ds, j to third p of last r, 5 ds, 2 p sep by 5 ds, 4 ds, cl) twice, turn, ch 4 ds, j to third p of last r, 14 ds, p, 4 ds, j to bottom of lr, ch 7 ds, j in first p of ch (first row), 3 ds, j in next p of same ch, 6 ds, p, 5 ds, turn, r 3 ds, p, 3 ds, j to p of ch, 3 ds, cl, (turn, ch 4 ds, turn, r 3 ds, 3 p sep by 3 ds, 3 ds, cl) twice, turn, ch 5 ds, j to p of opposite ch, 6 ds, j in p of next ch (last row), 3 ds, j in next p of same ch, 7 ds, turn, lr 12 ds, p, 12 ds, cl, turn, ch 4 ds, j to second p of last r, repeat from * around. Tie and cut.

SMALL MEDALLION (Top Row, Right)
(2 Shuttles)

Center: (R 10 ds, p, 10 ds, cl) 4 times. Tie and cut.

1st row: Join first shuttle thread to p of r, (ch 4 ds, 5 p sep by 2 ds, 4 ds, j to next p) 4 times. Tie and cut.

2d row: R 4 ds, 3 p sep by 4 ds, 4 ds, cl, *turn, ch 7 ds, p, 7 ds, p, 4 ds, j to third p of r, 7 ds, j to first p of ch (last row), 7 ds, p, 4 ds, j to opposite p, 7 ds, p, 7 ds, turn, r 4 ds, j to p of ch, 4 ds, j to third p of same ch of last row, 4 ds, p, 4 ds, cl, turn, ch 7 ds, p, 7 ds, p, 4 ds, j to third p of r, 7 ds, j to fifth p of same ch (last row), 7 ds, p, 4 ds, j to opposite p, 7 ds, p, 7 ds, turn, r 4 ds, j to opposite p of ch, 4 ds, 2 p sep by 4 ds, 4 ds, cl, repeat from * around. Tie and cut.

ROUND MEDALLION (Middle Row, Left)
(2 Shuttles)

Center: R 2 ds, 8 p sep by 3 ds. Tie and cut.

1st row: *Sr 3 ds, j to a p of center r, 3 ds, cl, ch 4 ds, p, 4 ds. Repeat from * around. Tie and cut.

2d row: *R 4 ds, j to p of ch of last row, 4 ds, cl, ch 6 ds, p, 6 ds. Repeat from * around. Tie and cut.

3d row: *R 4 ds, j to p of ch of last row, 4 ds, cl, ch 4 ds, p, 4 ds, r 4 ds, j to same p of same ch of last row, 4 ds, cl, ch 10 ds, p, 10 ds. Repeat from * around. Tie and cut.

4th row: Lr 9 ds, p, 7 ds, j to p of ch of last row, 7 ds, p, 9 ds, cl, * r 4 ds, 3 p sep by 4 ds, 4 ds, cl, ch 10 ds, r 4 ds, j to third p of lr, 6 ds, p, 4 ds, cl, ch 10 ds, lr 9 ds, j to second p of last r, 7 ds, j to p of next ch, 7 ds, p, 9 ds, cl. Repeat from * around. Tie and cut.

LARGE POINTED MEDALLION (Middle Row, Right)
(2 Shuttles)

Center Motif: (R 12 ds, p, 12 ds, cl) 4 times. Make 8 motifs like center one, j one to each p of center motif, and j one between each around the edge.

Next row: R 5 ds, p, 5 ds, j to p of motif, 5 ds, p, 5 ds, cl, r 5 ds, j to third p of last r, 5 ds, 2 p sep by 5 ds, 5 ds, cl, *turn, ch 9 ds, p, 7 ds, turn, r 5 ds, 3 p, sep by 5 ds, 5 ds, cl, (r 5 ds, j to third p of last r, 5 ds, 2 p sep by 5 ds, 5 ds, cl) twice, turn, ch 7 ds, j to p of opposite ch, 9 ds, turn, r 5 ds, 3 p sep by 5 ds, 5 ds, cl, r 5 ds, j to third p of last r, 5 ds, j to p of next motif, 5 ds, p, 5 ds, cl. Tie and cut. R 5 ds, p, 5 ds, j to same p of motif with last r, 5 ds, p, 5 ds, cl, r 5 ds, j to third p of last r, 5 ds, j to second p of opposite r, 5 ds, p, 5 ds, cl. Repeat from * around.

LARGE SQUARE MEDALLION (Bottom Row, Left)
(2 Shuttles)

Center: (R 9 ds, p, 9 ds, cl, turn, ch 12 ds, turn) 4 times. Tie and cut.

1st row: R 6 ds, 3 p sep by 6 ds, 6 ds, cl, *turn, ch 9 ds, p, 9 ds, turn, r 6 ds, j to third p of last r, 6 ds, 2 p sep by 6 ds, 6 ds, cl, turn, ch 9 ds, p, 9 ds, turn, r 6 ds, j to third p of last r, 6 ds, j to p of center, 6 ds, p, 6 ds, cl, turn, ch 9 ds, p, 9 ds, turn, r 6 ds, j to third p of last r, 6 ds, j to same p of center, 6 ds, p, 6 ds, cl, turn, ch 9 ds, p, 9 ds, turn, r 6 ds, j to third p of last r, 6 ds, 2 p sep by 6 ds, 6 ds, cl, repeat from * around, j last r to first r. Tie and cut.

Make 4 small motifs and j to second row as follows: R 5 ds, j to p of ch between the two r of center, 5 ds, 2 p sep by 5 ds, 5 ds, cl, r 5 ds, j to third p of last r, 6 ds, p, 6 ds, p, 5 ds, cl, r 5 ds, j to third p of last r, 5 ds, p, 5 ds, j to p of next ch (last row), 5 ds, cl. Tie and cut, sk 2 ch between each small motif.

2d row: R 5 ds, 3 p sep by 5 ds, 5 ds, cl, r 5 ds, j to third p of last r, 6 ds, j to first p of small motif, 6 ds, p, 5 ds, cl, r 5 ds, j to third p of last r, 5 ds, 2 p sep by 5 ds, 5 ds, cl, turn, ch 12 ds, p, 12 ds, turn, r 5 ds, p, 5 ds, j to center p of last r, 5 ds, p, 5 ds, cl, r 5 ds, j to third p of last r, 6 ds, j to center p of small motif, 6 ds, p, 5 ds, cl, r 5 ds, j to third p of last r, 5 ds, 2 p sep by 5 ds, 5 ds, cl, *turn, ch 14 ds, p, 14 ds, turn, r 5 ds, p, 5 ds, j to center p of last r, 5 ds, p, 5 ds, cl, r 5 ds, j to third p of last r, 6 ds, j to same with last shamrock, 6 ds, p, 5 ds, cl, r 5 ds, j to third p of last r, 5 ds, 2 p sep by 5 ds, 5 ds, cl, (turn, ch 12 ds, p, 12 ds, turn, r 5 ds, p, 5 ds, j to center p of last r, 5 ds, p, 5 ds, cl, r 5 ds, j to third p of last r, 6 ds, j to next p (last row), 6 ds, p, 5 ds, cl) 5 times. Repeat from * around. Tie and cut.

LARGE ROUND MEDALLION (Bottom Row, Right)
(2 Shuttles)

Center: (R 12 ds, p, 12 ds, cl) 4 times. Tie and cut.

1st row: *R 12 ds, j to p of a center r, 12 ds, cl, turn, ch 4 ds, 3 p sep by 3 ds, 4 ds, turn, r 12 ds, j to p of same r, 12 ds, cl, turn, ch 4 ds, 3 p sep by 3 ds, 4 ds, turn, repeat from * around. Tie and cut.

2d row: Lr 4 ds, 3 p sep by 4 ds, 4 ds, cl, turn, sp (¼-inch), sr 4 ds, 3 p sep by 3 ds, 4 ds, cl, *(turn, sp, lr 4 ds, j to third p of last lr, 4 ds, 2 p sep by 4 ds, 4 ds, cl, turn, sp, sr 4 ds, j to third p of last sr, 3 ds, j to p of ch (last row), 3 ds, p, 4 ds, cl) 3 times, turn, sp, lr 4 ds, j to third p of last lr, 4 ds, 2 p sep by 4 ds, 4 ds, cl, turn, sp, sr 4 ds, j to third p of last sr, 3 ds, 2 p sep by 3 ds, 4 ds, cl, repeat from * around. Tie and cut.

3d row: *R 3 ds, j to p of lr of last row, 3 ds, cl, ch 5 ds. p, 5 ds. Repeat from * around.

Detail and Directions on Page 19

RECTANGULAR LUNCHEON SET

Continued from Page 9

turn, ch 6 ds, 3 p sep by 2 ds, turn, r 6 ds, j to center p of ch (last row), 6 ds, cl. Repeat from * around, j four r to center motif with ch between, as in first corner. Tie and cut.

4th row: R 3 ds, 3 p sep by 3 ds, 3 ds, cl, turn, ch 5 ds, p, 2 ds, j to first p at left of corner ch (last row), 2 ds, 2 p sep by 2 ds, 5 ds, turn, r 3 ds, p, 3 ds, j to center p of last r, 3 ds, p, 3 ds, cl, turn, ch 2 ds, p, 2 ds, turn, r 3 ds, 3 p sep by 3 ds, 3 ds, cl, turn, ch 5 ds, j to p of opposite ch, 2 ds, p, 2 ds, j to third p of same ch (last row), 2 ds, p, 5 ds, turn. * r 3 ds, p, 3 ds, j to center p of last r, 3 ds, p, 3 ds, cl, turn, ch 3 ds, turn, r 3 ds, 3 p sep by 3 ds, 3 ds, cl, turn, ch 5 ds, p, 2 ds, j to center p of next ch, 2 ds, p, 5 ds, turn. Repeat from * around, working each corner same as first corner. Tie and cut.

5th row: R 3 ds, p, 3 ds, j in p with the two r to left of a corner, 3 ds, p, 3 ds, cl, turn, ch 5 ds, 3 p sep by 2 ds, 5 ds, turn, r 3 ds, p, 3 ds, j in same p with last r, 3 ds, p, 3 ds, cl, r 3 ds, 3 p sep by 3 ds, 3 ds, cl, turn, ch 5 ds, 3 p sep by 2 ds, 5 ds, turn (r 3 ds, p, 3 ds, j in center p of last r, 3 ds, p, 3 ds, cl, turn, ch 5 ds, 3 p sep by 2 ds, 5 ds, turn) twice, r 3 ds, p, 3 ds, j to same p with last three r, 3 ds, p, 3 ds, cl, * r 3 ds, p, 3 ds, j to p with next 2 r of last row, 3 ds, p, 3 ds, cl, turn, ch 5 ds, 3 p sep by 2 ds, 5 ds, turn, r 3 ds, p, 3 ds, j in same p with last r, 3 ds, p, 3 ds, cl.

turn, ch 3 ds, turn. Repeat from * around, working each corner same as first corner. Tie and cut.

6th row: R 2 ds, 7 p sep by 2 ds, 2 ds, cl, turn, ch 9 ds, turn, r 2 ds, 3 p sep by 2 ds, 2 ds, j to center p of ch to left of corner of last row, 2 ds, 3 p sep by 2 ds, 2 ds, cl, turn, ch 9 ds, turn, r 2 ds, 7 p sep by 2 ds, 2 ds, cl, turn, ch 9 ds, turn, r 2 ds, 3 p sep by 2 ds, 2 ds, j to first p of next ch of last row, 2 ds, 3 p sep by 2 ds, 2 ds, cl, turn, ch 9 ds, turn, r 2 ds, 7 p sep by 2 ds, 2 ds, cl, turn, ch 9 ds, turn, r 2 ds, 3 p sep by 2 ds, 2 ds, j to third p of same ch, 2 ds, 3 p sep by 2 ds, 2 ds, cl, * turn, ch 9 ds, turn, r 2 ds, 7 p sep by 2 ds, 2 ds, cl, turn, ch 9 ds, turn, r 2 ds, 3 p sep by 2 ds, 2 ds, j to center p of next ch, 2 ds, 3 p sep by 2 ds, 2 ds, cl. Repeat from * around, working each corner same as first corner. Tie and cut.

7th row: R 3 ds, 3 p sep by 3 ds, 3 ds, cl, turn, ch 5 ds, p, 2 ds, j to 3 p of corner r, 2 ds, p, 5 ds, turn, p, 3 ds, j in center p of last r, 3 ds, p, 3 ds, cl, r 3 ds, 3 p sep by 2 ds, 3 ds, cl, turn, ch 5 ds, p, 2 ds, j in fifth p of corner r, 2 ds, p, 5 ds, * turn, r 3 ds, p, 3 ds, j in center p of last r, 3 ds, p, 3 ds, cl, turn, ch 3 ds, turn, r 3 ds, 3 p sep by 3 ds, 3 ds, cl, turn, ch 5 ds, 3 p sep by 2 ds, 5 ds, turn, r 3 ds, p, 3 ds, j in center p of last r, 3 ds, p, 3 ds, cl, turn, ch 3 ds, turn, r 3 ds, 3 p sep by 3 ds, 3 ds, cl, turn,

Continued on Page 27

— 18 —

Luncheon Set

Shown on Pages 16 and 17

LARGE DOILY

For Medallions:

Center: R 7 ds, 7 p sep by 2 ds, 7 ds, cl, (r 7 ds, j to seventh p of last r, 2 ds, 6 p sep by 2 ds, 7 ds, cl) 4 times, j last r to first r. Tie and cut.

1st row: (Lr 6 ds, 7 p sep by 2 ds, 6 ds, cl), 3 times, j r by first and last p, turn, ch 6 ds, turn, sr 2 ds, 2 p sep by 2 ds, 2 ds, j to third p of lr of center, 2 ds, cl, * sr 2 ds, j to next p of same lr, 2 ds, 2 p sep by 2 ds, 2 ds, cl, turn, ch 6 ds, turn, lr 6 ds, 3 p sep by 2 ds, 2 ds, j to center p of last lr, 2 ds, 3 p sep by 2 ds, 6 ds, cl, (lr 6 ds, j to seventh p of last lr, 2 ds, 6 p sep by 2 ds, 6 ds, cl) twice, turn, ch 6 ds, turn, sr 2 ds, p, 2 ds

j to center p of last sr, 2 ds, p, 2 ds, cl, sr 2 ds, 3 p sep by 2 ds, 2 ds, cl, turn, ch 6 ds, turn, lr 6 ds, 3 p sep by 2 ds, 2 ds, j to center p of last lr, 2 ds, 3 p sep by 2 ds, 6 ds, cl, (lr 6 ds, j to seventh p of last lr, 2 ds, 6 p sep by 2 ds, 6 ds, cl) twice, turn, ch 6 ds, turn, sr 2 ds, p, 2 ds, j to center p of last sr, 2 ds, j to third p of next lr of center, 2 ds, cl, repeat from * around. Tie and cut.

2nd row: (Lr 5 ds, 7 p sep by 2 ds, 5 ds, cl) 3 times, j r by first and last p, * turn, ch 5 ds, 7 p sep by 2 ds, 5 ds, turn, sr 3 ds, p, 3 ds, j to third p of last lr, 3 ds, p, 3 ds, cl, turn, ch 4 ds, turn, sr 3 ds, j to third p of sr, 3 ds, j to next p of last lr, 3 ds, p, 3 ds, cl, turn,

Continued on Page 29

Directions for Medallions

Shown on Opposite Page

LARGE MEDALLION (1st Column, Top)

(2 Shuttles)

1st row: R 4 ds, 3 p sep by 4 ds, 4 ds, cl, (ch 8 ds, p, 8 ds, r 4 ds, j to third p of last r, 4 ds, 2 p sep by 4 ds, 4 ds, cl) 8 times, j last r to first r, ch 8 ds, p, 8 ds. Tie and cut.

2d row: R 4 ds, 3 p sep by 4 ds, 4 ds, cl, * ch 8 ds, p, 8 ds, r 4 ds, j to third p of last r, 4 ds, j to p of ch of last row, 4 ds, p, 4 ds, cl, ch 8 ds, p, 8 ds, r 4 ds, j to third p of last r, 4 ds, 2 p sep by 4 ds, 4 ds, cl. Repeat from * around. Tie and cut.

3d row: R 9 ds, lp, 9 ds, cl, (ch 7 ds, 5 p, 7 ds, r 9 ds, j to lp of first r, 9 ds, cl) 3 times, ch 7 ds, 2 p, j to p of ch, 2 p, 7 ds, * r 9 ds, lp, 9 ds, cl, ch 7 ds, p, j to fourth p of opposite ch, 4 p, 7 ds, (r 9 ds, j to lp of first r, 9 ds, cl. ch 7 ds, 5 p, 7 ds) twice, r 9 ds, j to lp, 9 ds, cl, ch 7 ds, 2 p, sk 1 ch of last row, j in p of next ch, 2 p, 7 ds. Repeat from * around. Tie and cut.

ROUND MEDALLION (1st Column, Center)

(2 Shuttles)

1st row: R 3 ds, 3 p sep by 3 ds, 3 ds, cl, (turn, ch 7 ds, p, 7 ds, turn, r 3 ds, j to third p of last r, 3 ds, 2 p sep by 3 ds, 3 ds, cl), 9 times, turn, ch 7 ds, p, 7 ds. Tie and cut.

2d row: R 3 ds, 3 p sep by 3 ds, 3 ds, cl, * turn, sp (¼ inch) sr 4 ds, p, 4 ds, cl, turn, sp, r 3 ds, j to third p of r, 3 ds, 2 p sep by 3 ds, 3 ds, cl, turn, sp, lr 3 ds, j to p of sr, 3 ds, 2 p sep by 3 ds, 3 ds, cl, turn, sp, r 3 ds, j to third p of r, 3 ds, j to p of ch, 3 ds, p, 3 ds, cl, turn, sp, sr 4 ds, j to third p of lr, 4 ds, cl, turn, sp, r 3 ds, j to third p of r, 3 ds, 2 p sep by 3 ds, 3 ds, cl. Repeat from * around. Tie and cut.

SQUARE MEDALLION (1st Column, Bottom)

(2 Shuttles)

Small motifs: (R 6 ds, 3 p sep by 5 ds, 6 ds, cl) 4 times, j r together by first and third p. Tie and cut.
Make four more motifs, j one to each center p of r of first motif.

Edge: * R 5 ds, p, 5 ds, j to p of r opposite one j to center motif, 5 ds, p, 5 ds, cl, ch 5 ds, 3 p sep by 5 ds, 5 ds, r 5 ds, j to third p of last r, 5 ds, j to same p with last r, 5 ds, p, 5 ds, cl, ch 5 ds, 3 p sep by 5 ds, 5 ds, (r 4 ds, j to third p of last r, 5 ds, 2 p sep by 5 ds, 5 ds, cl, ch 5 ds, 3 p sep by 5 ds, 5 ds) 3 times. Repeat from * around. Tie and cut.

SMALL MEDALLION (2d Column, Top)

(2 Shuttles)

1st row: (R 3 ds, 5 p sep by 3 ds, 3 ds, cl, turn, ch 3 ds, 5 p sep by 3 ds, 3 ds, turn) 7 times, j r by second and fourth p. Tie and cut.

2d row: R 8 ds, p, 6 ds, p, 2 ds, cl, * r 2 ds, j to last p of last r, 5 ds, 3 p, 5 ds, p, 2 ds, cl, r 2 ds, j to last p of last r, 6 ds, p, 8 ds, cl, turn, ch 6 ds, j to fourth p of a ch of last row, 6 ds, turn, r 4 ds, j to last p of last r, 3 ds, 3 p, 3 ds, p, 4 ds, cl, turn, ch 6 ds, j to second p of same ch of last row, 6 ds, turn, r 8 ds, j to last p of last r, 6 ds, p, 2 ds, cl. Repeat from * around. Tie and cut.

OBLONG MEDALLION (2d Column, 2d from Top)

(2 Shuttles)

Make 4 motifs as follows: R 3 ds, 3 p sep by 3 ds, 3 ds, cl, (turn, ch 5 ds, p, 5 ds, turn, r 3 ds, j to third p of last r, 3 ds, 2 p sep by 3 ds, 3 ds, cl) 5 times, turn, ch 5 ds, p, 5 ds. Tie and cut.

Join the motifs as in illustration.

Edge: R 4 ds, j to center p of center motif, 4 ds, cl, turn, ch 4 ds, p, 4 ds, * turn, r 4 ds, j in same p with last r, 4 ds, cl, turn, (ch 6 ds, p, 6 ds, turn, r 4 ds, j to p of next ch, 4 ds, cl) 3 times, turn, ch 4 ds, p, 4 ds, turn, r 4 ds, j in same p with last r, 4 ds, cl, (turn, ch 6 ds, p 6 ds, turn, r 4 ds, j in p of next ch, 4 ds, cl) 4 times, turn, ch 4 ds, p, 4 ds, turn, repeat from * around. Tie and cut.

POINTED MEDALLION (2d Column, 3d from Top)

(2 Shuttles)

(R 3 ds, p) 5 times, 3 ds, cl, ch 9 ds, (r 4 ds, p) 3 times, 4 ds, cl. Ch 5 ds, p, 4 ds, r 4 ds, j to last p of last r, (4 ds, p) twice, 4 ds, cl, ch 4 ds, p, 3 ds, r 4 ds, j to last p of last r, (4 ds, p) twice, 4 ds, cl ch 3 ds, r 3 ds, j to last p of last r, (3 ds, p) 4 times, 3 ds, cl, ch 3 ds, r 4 ds, j to last p of last r, (4 ds, p) twice, 4 ds, cl, ch 3 ds, j to p of third ch made, 4 ds, r 4 ds, j to last p of last r, (4 ds, p) twice, 4 ds, cl, ch 4 ds, j to p of second ch made, 5 ds, r 4 ds, j to last p of last r, (4 ds, p) twice, 4 ds, cl, ch 9 ds. Repeat from beginning, making 6 points, j center r.

SMALL MEDALLION (2d Column, Bottom)

(2 Shuttles)

Center: R 5 p sep by 3 ds, cl, ch 3 ds, 3 p sep by 3 ds, 3 ds, repeat r and ch 4 times, j each new r to preceding r by second p. Tie and cut.

1st row: * Sr 3 ds, j to p of center, 3 ds, cl, ch 3 ds, 3 p sep by 3 ds, 3 ds. Repeat from * all around. Tie and cut.

2d row: Sr 3 ds, j to center p of ch of first row, 3 ds, cl, ch 8 ds, p, 8 ds. Repeat r and ch all around. Tie and cut

LARGE ROUND MEDALLION (3d Column, Top)

(1 Shuttle)

R 12 p sep by 3 ds, cl. Tie and cut.

1st row: Lr 6 ds, 9 p sep by 3 ds, 6 ds, cl, * turn, sp (¼ inch), sr 6 s, j to p of center r, 6 ds, cl, turn, sp, lr 6 ds, j to ninth p of last lr, 3 ds, 8 p sep by 3 ds, 6 ds, cl. Repeat from * around. Tie and cut.

2d row: Made like first row, j 2 sr to third and fifth p of each lr of last row.

CLOVER MEDALLION (3d Column, Center)

(2 Shuttles)

Center Motif: (R 5 ds, 3 p sep by 5 ds, 5 ds, cl) 4 times, j r by first and third p. Tie and cut.

Continued on Page 28

Edgings

For simple luncheon sets, chair sets, bedroom sets, made of linen, an effective touch is added by using an edging, either simple or elaborate, and made of crochet cotton in either No. 50, 30, or 10, depending on the weight of the linen used. A medallion inserted in each of the corners makes a set unusual and one is amply repaid for the extra work.

EDGING No. 1

*R 8 ds, p, 3 ds, 3 p sep by 2 ds, 3 ds, p, 8 ds. Do not close entirely, but leave 3-8 of an inch open between ends. Repeat from * for desired length, always j by first p.

EDGING No. 2
(2 Shuttles)

R 5 ds, 3 p sep by 3 ds, 5 ds, cl, r 5 ds, j in third p of last r, 3 ds, 2 p sep by 3 ds, 5 ds, cl, * 1r 5 ds, j to p of last r, 3 ds, 4 p sep by 3 ds, 5 ds, cl, r 5 ds, j to fifth p of 1r, 3 ds, 2 p sep by 3 ds, 5 ds, cl, turn, ch 7 ds, p, 2 ds, p, 7 ds, turn, r 5 ds, 3 p sep by 3 ds, 5 ds, cl, r 5 ds, j in third p of last r, 3 ds, j in center p of opposite r, 3 ds, p, 5 ds, cl. Repeat from *.

EDGING No. 3
(2 Shuttles)

*R 5 ds, p, 5 ds, cl, 1 ch 3 ds, 4 p sep by 3 ds, 3 ds, j to p of r, 3 ds, 4 p sep by 3 ds, 3 ds, j in first p below sr on opposite side, 3 ds, 3 p sep by 3 ds, 3 ds, turn, r 5 ds, j in opposite p on 1 ch, 5 ds, cl. Repeat from *.

EDGING No. 4
(2 Shuttles)

*(R 3 ds, p) 3 times, 4 ds, cl, ch 8 ds, r 6 ds, j to third p of first r, 6 ds, cl, ch 8 ds, r 4 ds, j to third p of first r, 3 ds, p, 3 ds, p, 4 ds, cl, ch 8 ds, r 6 ds, j to last p of center r, 5 ds, cl, ch 8 ds, r 4 ds, j to p of center r, 3 ds, p, 3 ds, p, 4 ds, cl, ch 7 ds. Repeat from * for desired length.

EDGING No. 5
(2 Shuttles)

R 3 ds, 3 p sep by 2 ds, 3 ds, cl, * turn, ch 4 ds, 3 p sep by 2 ds, 5 ds, p, 5 ds, turn, r 3 ds, p, 2 ds, j in center p of last r, 2 ds, p, 3 ds, cl, turn, ch 5 ds, 3 p sep by 2 ds, 5 ds, r 3 ds, 3 p sep by 2 ds, 3 ds, cl, ch 5 ds, j to p on opposite ch, 5 ds, 3 p sep by 2 ds, 4 ds, turn, r 3 ds, p, 2 ds, j in center p of last r, 2 ds, p, 3 ds, cl. Repeat from *.

EDGING No. 6
(2 Shuttles)

R 5 ds, 3 p sep by 5 ds, 5 ds, cl, ch 10 ds, p, 10 ds, * r 5 ds, p, 5 ds, j to second p of preceding r, 5 ds, p, 5 ds, cl, r 5 ds, j to p of preceding r, 3 ds, 5 p sep by 2 ds, 3 ds, p, 5 ds, cl, r 5 ds, 3 p sep by 5 ds, 5 ds, cl, ch 10 ds, p, 10 ds. Repeat from * for desired length.

EDGING No. 7
(2 Shuttles)

*R 3 ds, 3 p sep by 3 ds, 3 ds, cl, turn, ch 10 ds, r 2 ds, 3 p sep by 2 ds, 2 ds, cl, (r 2 ds, j to third p of last r, 2 ds, 2 p sep by 2 ds, 2 ds, cl) twice, turn, ch 10 ds, r 3 ds, p, 3 ds, j to center p of opposite r, 3 ds, p, 3 ds, cl. Repeat from * for desired length.

EDGING No. 8

R 3 ds, 3 p sep by 2 ds, 3 ds, cl, * turn, ch 5 ds, p, 5 ds, turn, r 2 ds, p, 2 ds, j to third p of last r, 2 ds, p, 2 ds, cl, r 2 ds, 3 p sep by 2 ds, 2 ds, cl, turn, ch 5 ds, p, 5 ds, turn, r 3 ds, j to center p of last r, 2 ds, 2 p sep by 2 ds, 3 ds, cl. Repeat from * for desired length.

EDGING No. 9
(2 Shuttles)

R 3 ds, 3 p with 3 ds between, 3 ds, cl, * ch 7 ds, p, 7 ds, r 3 ds, j to third p of last r, 3 ds, p, 3 ds, p, 3 ds, cl. Repeat from * for desired length.

EDGING No. 10
(2 Shuttles)

R 1 ds, 2 p with 1 ds between, 1 ds, 1 lp, 1 ds, 4 p with 1 ds between, 1 ds, 1 lp, 1 ds, 2 p with 1 ds between, 1 ds, cl, * ch 7 ds, p, 7 ds, r 1 ds, p, 1 ds, p, 1 ds, j to second lp of last r, 1 ds, 4 p with 1 ds between, lp, 1 ds, 2 p with 1 ds between, 1 ds, cl. Repeat from * for desired length.

EDGING No. 11
(2 Shuttles)

* R 3 ds, 9 p sep by 2 ds, 3 ds, cl, turn, ch 6 ds, 3 p sep by 2 ds, 6 ds, j in center p of r. Repeat from *.

Edgings

EDGING No. 12
(2 Shuttles)

R 3 ds, 3 p sep by 3 ds, 3 ds, cl, *
turn, ch 5 ds, 3 p sep by 2 ds, 5 ds,
p, 5 ds, turn, r 3 ds, p, 3 ds, j in third
p of last r, 3 ds, p, 3 ds, cl; r 3 ds, j
to last p of last r, 3 ds, 2 p sep by 3
ds, 3 ds, cl, turn, ch 10 ds, turn, r 4
ds, j to third p of last r, 2 ds, 4 p
sep by 2 ds, 4 ds, cl, r 4 ds, j to fifth
p of last r, 2 ds, 6 p sep by 2 ds, 4
ds, cl, r 4 ds, j to last p of last r, 2
ds, 4 p sep by 2 ds, 4 ds, cl, turn, ch
10 ds, turn, sr 3 ds, j to last p of
last r, 3 ds, 2 p sep by 3 ds, 3 ds,
cl, r 3 ds, j to last p of last r, 3 ds,
2 p sep by 3 ds, 3 ds, cl, turn, ch 5
ds, j to p of opposite ch, 6 ds, p, 5
ds, r 3 ds, j to center p of last r, 3
ds, 2 p sep by 3 ds, 3 ds, cl. Repeat
from *.

EDGING No. 13
(2 Shuttles)

R 7 p, cl, 1 ch 6 ds, 3 p sep by 2 ds,
6 ds, p, 6 ds, j in second p of last r,
6 ds, p, 8 ds, turn, r 7 p, cl, *(turn,
ch 4 ds, 1 lp, j in second p of last
r, 5 p, cl) twice, 1 ch 8 ds, j in p of
opposite 1 ch, 6 ds, p, 6 ds, j in p on
opposite 1 ch, 6 ds, 3 p sep by 2 ds,
6 ds, turn, r 1 p, j to p on opposite
1 ch, 5 p, cl, turn, ch 6 ds, 3 p sep
by 2 ds, 6 ds, p, 6 ds, j in second p of
last r, 6 ds, p, 8 ds, turn, r 3 p, j
in fourth p of opposite r, 3 p, cl. Repeat from *.

EDGING No. 14
(2 Shuttles)

(R 12 ds, p, 12 ds, cl) twice, * turn,
ch 11 ds, r 12 ds, j in p of last r, 12
ds, cl, (r 12 ds, p, 12 ds, cl) twice,
turn, ch 11 ds, r 12 ds, j in p of last
r, 12 ds, cl, r 12 ds, p, 12 ds, cl, repeat from * for desired length. Tie
and cut.
Heading: Join thread in p of r, *
ch 6 ds, 3 p sep by 2 ds, 6 ds, j in
next p. Repeat from * across.

EDGING No. 15
(2 Shuttles)

Lr 4 ds, 2 p sep by 4 ds, 5 ds, 2
p sep by 5 ds, 4 ds, p, 4 ds, cl, *
ch 8 ds, p, 8 ds, sr 6 ds, j to fifth
p of lr, 6 ds, cl, ch 6 ds, sr 6 ds, j
to fourth p of lr, 6 ds, cl, ch 6 ds,
sr 6 ds, p, 4 ds, p, 4 ds, cl, sr 4 ds,
j to last p of last sr, 5 ds, p, 5 ds,
p, 4 ds, cl, sr 4 ds, j to last p of
last r, 4 ds, p, 6 ds, cl, (ch 6 ds, sr
6 ds, p, 6 ds, cl) twice, j thread to
opposite sr, ch 8 ds, p, 8 ds, lr 4 ds,
j to last p of last r, 4 ds, j to p of next
sr, 5 ds, p, 5 ds, p, 4 ds, p, 4 ds,
cl. Repeat from * for desired length.

EDGING No. 16
(2 Shuttles)

1st row: R 4 ds, 3 p sep by 4 ds,
4 ds, cl, * ch 8 ds, p, 8 ds, r 4 ds,

j to p of last r, 4 ds, 2 p sep by 4
ds, 4 ds, cl. Repeat from * for desired length.

2nd row—Medallion: R 5 ds, 3 p
sep by 5 ds, 5 ds. cl. Repeat 3 times,
j first p of each r to last p of preceding r, cl. Tie and cut. Make
enough medallions to j to every other
r of first row, j medallions together
as in illustration.

3rd row: Make same medallion as
for second row. Join first medallion
to second medallion on second row.
* Sk two medallions, j a medallion
to next medallion of last row. Repeat
from * across.

4th row: R 4 ds, j to p of first medallion of second row, 4 ds, 2 p sep
by 4 ds, 4 ds, cl, * (ch 6 ds, p, 6 ds,
r 4 ds, j to last p of last r, 4 ds, j
to next p of medallion on third row,
4 ds, p, 4 ds, cl, ch 6 ds, p, 6 ds, r 4
ds, j to third p of last r, 4 ds, 2 p
sep by 4 ds, 4 ds, cl) twice, ch 6 ds,
p, 6 ds, r 4 ds, j to last p of last r,
4 ds, j to next p of medallion, 4 ds,
p, 4 ds, cl, ch 6 ds, p, 6 ds, r 4 ds,
j to last p of last r, 4 ds, p, 4 ds, j
to p of next free medallion of second row, 4 ds, cl, ch 12 ds, r 4 ds, j
to p of next medallion of second row,
4 ds, 2 p sep by 4 ds, 4 ds, cl. Repeat from * across.

DEEP POINTED EDGING No. 17

* R 4 ds, p, 5 ds, p, 4 ds, cl, ch 6 ds,
p, 6 ds, p, 6 ds, r 4 ds, j to p of
last r, 5 ds, p, 4 ds, cl, ch 6 ds, r 4
ds, p, 5 ds, p, 4 ds, cl, ch 6 ds, r 4
ds, p, 5 ds, p, 4 ds, cl, ch 6 ds, j to
p of ch opposite, 6 ds, p, 6 ds, r 4
ds, j to p of last r, 5 ds, p, 4 ds, cl,
ch 6 ds, p, 6 ds, p, 6 ds, r 4 ds, j to
p of last r, 5 ds, p, 4 ds, cl, ch 6 ds,
p, 6 ds, p, 6 ds, r 4 ds, j to p of last
r, 5 ds, j to p of r opposite, 4 ds, cl,
ch 6 ds, r 4 ds, j to p of opposite r,
5 ds, p, 4 ds, cl, ch 6 ds, r 4 ds, p,
5 ds, p, 4 ds, cl, ch 6 ds, j to p of
last r, 5 ds, p, 4 ds, cl, ch 6 ds, r 4
ds, p, 5 ds, p, 4 ds, cl, ch 6 ds, r 4
ds, p, 5 ds, p, 4 ds, cl, ch 6 ds, j to
p of ch opposite, 6 ds, p, 6 ds, r 4
ds, j to p of last r, 5 ds, p, 4 ds,
cl, ch 6 ds, r 4 ds, p, 5 ds, p, 4 ds, cl,
ch 6 ds, r 4 ds, p, 5 ds, p, 4 ds, cl,
ch 6 ds, j to p of opposite ch, 6 ds,
j to p of opposite ch, 6 ds, r 4 ds,
j to p of last r, 5 ds, p, 4 ds, cl, ch 6
ds, j to p of ch opposite, 6 ds, p, 6 ds, r
4 ds, j to p of last r, 5 ds, p, 4 ds,
cl, ch 6 ds, p, 6 ds, p, 6 ds, r 4 ds, j
to p of last r, 5 ds, j to p of oppo-

Continued on Page 26

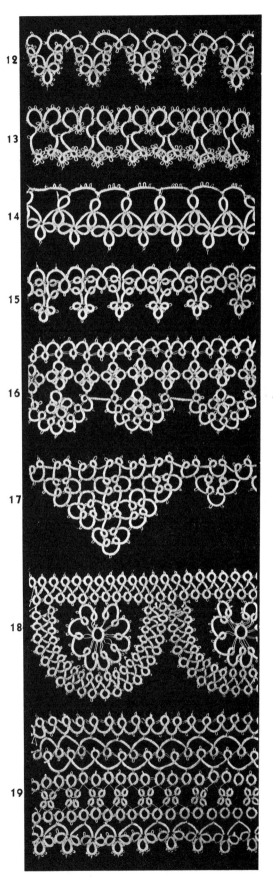

12

13

14

15

16

17

18

19

Edgings

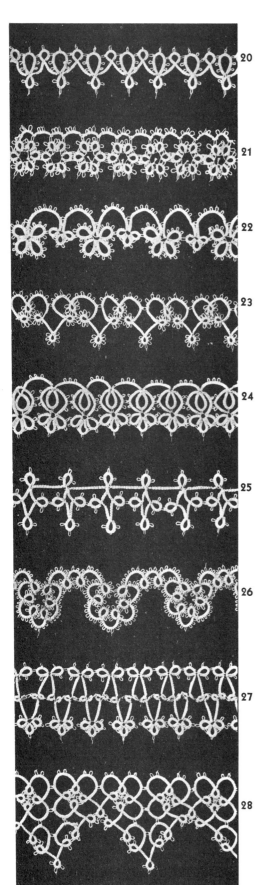

EDGING No. 20
(2 Shuttles)

Sr 4 ds, 3 p sep by 4 ds, 4 ds, cl, * turn, ch 8 ds, turn, lr 4 ds, 2 p sep by 4 ds, 4 ds, j to third p of sr, 4 ds, 4 p sep by 4 ds, 4 ds, cl, sr 4 ds, 3 p sep by 4 ds, 4 ds, cl, turn, ch 8 ds, turn, sr 4 ds, j to fifth p of lr, 4 ds, 2 p sep by 4 ds, 4 ds, cl. Repeat from * for desired length.

EDGING No. 21
(2 Shuttles)

Motif: R 2 ds, 5 p sep by 2 ds, 2 ds, cl, (r 2 ds, j to last p of last r, 2 ds, 4 p sep by 2 ds, 2 ds, cl) 5 times. Join fifth p of sixth r to first p of first r. Tie and cut.

Make motifs enough for length desired, j each together by the 3 p of first r of each motif.

Edge: Join thread in center p of r on side of motif. * Ch 3 ds, 3 p, 3 ds, j in center p of next r. Repeat from * across.

EDGING No. 22
(2 Shuttles)

R 3 ds, 7 p sep by 2 ds, 3 ds, cl, turn, l ch 6 ds, p, 6 ds, 5 p sep by 2 ds, 4 ds, p, 6 ds, * turn, sr 4 ds, j in fifth p of last r, 2 ds, p, 3 ds, cl, sr 3 ds, j in second p of last r, 2 ds, 3 p sep by 2 ds, 3 ds, cl, sr 3 ds, j to last p of last r, 2 ds, p, 4 ds, cl, l ch 6 ds, j to p of opposite l ch, 4 ds, 5 p sep by 2 ds, 6 ds, p, 6 ds, turn, r 3 ds, 4 p sep by 2 ds, 2 ds, j to p of last sr, 2 ds, 2 p sep by 2 ds, 3 ds, cl, (r 3 ds, j to last p of last r, 6 p sep by 2 ds, 3 ds, cl) 3 times, turn, ch 6 ds, j in p of opposite l ch, 6 ds, 5 p sep by 2 ds, 4 ds, p, 6 ds. Repeat from *.

FORGET-ME-NOT EDGING
No. 23
(2 Shuttles)

R 7 p, cl, turn, l ch 8 ds, 5 p sep by 2 ds, 3 ds, turn, *r 3 p, j in center p of last r, 3 p, cl, turn, l ch 3 ds, 5 p sep by 2 ds, 8 ds, turn, r 3 p, j in same p with last r, 3 p, cl, turn, ch 7 ds, turn, r 7 p, cl, turn, ch 7 ds, r 7 p, cl turn, l ch 8 ds, j in first p on opposite l ch, 2 ds, 4 p sep by 2 ds, 3 ds. Repeat from *.

POMEGRANATE EDGING
No. 24
(2 Shuttles)

R 12 ds, p, 12 ds, cl, turn, ch 6 ds, 3 p sep by 2 ds, 6 ds, * j in p of lr, r 5 ds, 3 p sep by 3 ds, 5 ds, cl, (r 5 ds, j in third p of last r, 3 ds, 2 p sep by 3 ds, 5 ds, cl) twice, j in p of lr, ch 5 ds, 3 p sep by 2 ds, 5 ds, j around lr at base, turn, ch 6 ds, 3 p sep by 2 ds, 6 ds, lr 12 ds, p, 12 ds, cl, ch 6 ds, p,

2 ds, j in center p of opposite ch, 2 ds, p, 6 ds. Repeat from *.

POINTED EDGING No. 25
(2 Shuttles)

R 4 ds, 3 p sep by 4 ds, 4 ds, cl, (turn, ch 6 ds, turn, r 4 ds, 3 p sep by 4 ds, 4 ds, cl) 3 times, * ch 6 ds, loop around first ch 6 ds, close to first r, turn, ch 12 ds, turn, r 4 ds, 3 p sep by 4 ds, 4 ds, cl, turn, ch 6 ds, turn, r 4 ds, p, 4 ds, j in center p of opposite r, 4 ds, p, 4 ds, cl, (turn, ch 6 ds, turn, r 4 ds, 3 p sep by 4 ds, 4 ds, cl) twice. Repeat from *.

EDGING No. 26
(2 Shuttles)

R 7 p sep by 2 ds, cl, * ch 7 p sep by 2 ds, r 7 p sep by 2 ds, cl, turn, ch 2 ds, 3 p sep by 2 ds, 2 ds, j to fifth p of opposite r, 2 ds, 3 p sep by 2 ds, 2 ds, (r 2 ds, 2 p sep by 2 ds, j to third p of opposite r, 2 ds, 4 p sep by 2 ds, 2 ds, cl, ch 2 ds, 7 p sep by 2 ds, 2 ds), four times, r 2 ds, 2 p sep by 2 ds, 2 ds, j to third p of last r, 2 ds, p, 2 ds, j to fifth p of opposite r, 2 ds, 2 p sep by 2 ds, 2 ds, cl, turn, ch 2 ds, 7 p sep by 2 ds, 2 ds, r 2 ds, 2 p sep by 2 ds, 2 ds, j to center p of opposite ch, 2 ds, 4 p sep by 2 ds, 2 ds, cl, turn, ch 2 ds, 4 p sep by 2 ds, 2 ds, r 2 ds, p, 2 ds, j to sixth p of last r, 2 ds, 5 p sep by 2 ds, 2 ds, cl. Repeat from *.

EDGING No. 27
(2 Shuttles)

(R 4 ds, 3 p sep by 4 ds, 4 ds, cl) twice, turn, ch 10 ds, (sr 3 ds, p, 3 ds, cl) twice, * ch 10 ds, r 3 ds, 3 p sep by 3 ds, 3 ds, cl, (r 3 ds, j to last p of last r, 3 ds, 2 p sep by 3 ds, 3 ds, cl) twice, turn, ch 10 ds, sr 3 ds, j in p of opposite sr, 3 ds, cl, sr 3 ds, p, 3 ds, cl, turn, ch 10 ds, turn, r 4 ds, p, 4 ds, j in center p of opposite r, 4 ds, p, 4 ds, cl, r 4 ds, 3 p sep by 4 ds, 4 ds, cl, turn, ch 10 ds, sr 3 ds, j in p of opposite sr, 3 ds, cl, sr 3 ds, p, 3 ds, cl, turn. Repeat from *.

WIDE POINTED EDGING
No. 28
(1¾ Inches Wide)
(2 Shuttles)

Sr 3 ds, 3 p sep by 2 ds, 3 ds, cl, ch 6 ds, p, 6 ds, p, 2 ds, p, 6 ds, sr 3 ds, j to third p of last r, 2 ds, p, 2 ds, p, 3 ds, cl, ch 6 ds, p, 2 ds, p, 6 ds, p, 6 ds, r 3 ds, j to third p of last r, 2 ds, p, 2 ds, p, 3 ds, cl, ch 6 ds, p, 6 ds, p, 6 ds, r 3 ds, j to third p of last r, 2 ds, p, 2 ds, j to first p of first r, 3 ds, cl, (ch 6 ds, r 3 ds, 3 p sep by 2 ds, 3 ds, cl) twice, * ch 6 ds, j in p on opposite ch, 6 ds, p, 6 ds, r 3 ds, p, 2 ds, j in center p of last r, 2 ds, p, 3

Continued on Page 26

Edgings

EDGING No. 29
(2 Shuttles)

R 4 ds, 3 p sep by 4 ds, 4 ds, cl, turn, 1 ch 3 ds, 5 p sep by 3 ds, 8 ds, turn, r 4 ds, p, 4 ds, j in center p of last r, 4 ds, p, 4 ds, cl, *turn, ch 5 ds, turn, r 4 ds, 3 p sep by 4 ds, 4 ds, cl, turn, ch 5 ds, turn, r 4 ds, 3 p sep by 4 ds, 4 ds, cl, turn, 1 ch 8 ds, j in first p on opposite 1 ch, 2 ds, 4 p sep by 2 ds, 3 ds, turn, r 4 ds, p, 4 ds, j in center p of last r, 4 ds, p, 4 ds, cl, turn, 1 ch 3 ds, 5 p sep by 2 ds, 8 ds, turn, r 4 ds, p, 4 ds, j in same p with last r, 4 ds, p, 4 ds, cl. Repeat from * for desired length.

EDGING No. 30
(2 Shuttles)

Lr 5 ds, 7 p sep by 2 ds, 5 ds, cl, *turn, ch 6 ds, 3 p sep by 2 ds, 6 ds, turn, sr 5 ds, p, 5 ds, cl, lr 5 ds, j in p of sr, 2 ds, j in last p of last lr, 2 ds, 5 p sep by 2 ds, 5 ds, cl, repeat from *.

EDGING No. 31
(2 Shuttles)

R 3 ds, 3 p sep by 3 ds, 3 ds, cl, turn, *(ch 5 ds, p) twice, 5 ds, turn, r 3 ds, 3 p sep by 3 ds, 3 ds, cl, turn, ch 5 ds, j to first p of opposite r, 3 ds, 2 p sep by 3 ds, 5 ds (turn, r 3 ds, p, 3 ds, j in center p of last r, 3 ds, p, 3 ds, cl, turn, ch 5 ds, 3 p sep by 3 ds, 5 ds) twice, r 3 ds, p, 3 ds, j in same p with other 3 r, 3 ds, p, 3 ds, cl, turn, ch 5 ds, turn, r 3 ds, p, 3 ds, j to second p of opposite ch, 3 ds, p, 3 ds, cl, turn, ch 5 ds, p, 5 ds, turn, r 3 ds, j to first p of opposite ch, 3 ds, 2 p sep by 3 ds, 3 ds, cl, repeat from *.

EDGING No. 32
(2 Shuttles)

R 12 p sep by 2 ds, cl, ch 5 ds, p, 5 ds, r 7 p sep by 2 ds, j second p to eleventh p of lr, cl, ch 5 ds, p, 5 ds, r 7 p sep by 2 ds, j second p to sixth p of preceding sr, cl, ch 5 ds, p, 5 ds. Repeat from beginning for desired length.

EDGING No. 33
(2 Shuttles)

R 5 ds, 3 p sep by 5 ds, 5 ds, cl, * turn, ch 7 ds, p, 7 ds, turn, r 5 ds, j in third p of last r, 5 ds, 2 p sep by 5 ds, 5 ds, cl. Repeat from *.

EDGING No. 34
(2 Shuttles)

*R Shuttle No. 1, 3 ds, 3 times, 3 ds, cl. Ch 5 ds, making st with Shut-

tle No. 2. Join thread of Shuttle No. 1 to last p of r, ch 3 ds, p, 3 ds, j to same p. Ch 5 ds, j to next p of r. Second r, Shuttle No. 1, 4 ds, p, 4 ds, r st 8 ds, cl. Repeat from *.

EDGING No. 35
(2 Shuttles)

R 5 ds, p, 6 ds, p, 6 ds, p, 5 ds, cl, *sp (⅛-inch), sr, 5 ds, p, 5 ds, cl, sp, r 5 ds, j to third p of first r, 6 ds, p, 6 ds, p, 5 ds, cl, sp, r 6 ds, j to p of sr, 5 ds, 3 p with 2 ds between, 5 ds, p, 6 ds, cl, sp, r 5 ds, j to third p of third r, 6 ds, p, 6 ds, p, 5 ds, cl, sp, sr 5 ds, j to p of lr, 5 ds, cl, sp, r 5 ds, j to p of fifth r, 6 ds, p, 6 ds, p, 5 ds, cl. Repeat from * for desired length.

EDGING No. 36
(2 Shuttles)

R 3 ds, 5 p sep by 2 ds, 3 ds, cl, (ch 4 ds, r 3 ds, j to fifth p of last r, 3 ds, 4 p sep by 2 ds, 3 ds, cl) twice, ch 5 ds, p, * 5 ds, 6 p sep by 2 ds, 5 ds, p, 5 ds, r 3 ds, 2 p sep by 2 ds, 2 ds, j to center p of last r, 2 ds, 2 p sep by 2 ds, 3 ds, cl (ch 4 ds, r 3 ds, j to fifth p of last r, 2 ds, 4 p sep by 2 ds, 3 ds, cl) twice, ch 5 ds, j to p of opposite ch. Repeat from *.

SCALLOPED EDGING No. 37
(2 Shuttles)

Begin sr, Shuttle No. 1, 3 ds, p, 1 ds, r st 3 ds, p, 1 ds, cl. Second sr, Shuttle No. 1, 1 ds, j to first p of first sr, 3 ds, p, 3 ds, p, 1 ds, cl. Third sr, Shuttle No. 2, 1 ds, j to last p of first sr, 3 ds, p ¼ inch, 3 ds, p, 1 ds, cl. R, Shuttle No. 1, 10 ds, r st 10 ds, cl (do not draw very taut) center r, Shuttle No 1, space, 1-16 inch (2 ds, p), 7 times, 2 ds, cl. Tie threads around thread between last 2 r. Ch 2 ds, making st with Shuttle No. 2. Join thread of Shuttle No. 1 to last p of center r, * ch 9 ds, sr, Shuttle No. 2, 1 ds, p, 3 ds, j to lp of last sr, twist p before j, 3 ds, p, 1 ds, cl. Second sr, 1 ds, j to p of sr, 3 ds, p, 3 ds, p, 1 ds, cl. Third sr, 1 ds, j to p of last r, 3 ds, p ¼ inch, 3 ds, p, 1 ds, cl. Ch 9 ds, j thread of Shuttle No. 1 to same p of center r. Ch 2 ds, j to next p of center r. *Repeat twice. R, Shuttle No. 1, 10 ds, r st 10 ds, cl, sr, Shuttle No. 2, 1 ds, p, 3 ds, j to lp of last sr, 3 ds, p, 1 ds, cl. Second sr, Shuttle No. 1, 1 ds, p, 3 ds, p, 3 ds, p, 1 ds, cl. Third sr, Shuttle No. 1, 1 ds, j to last p of last sr, 3 ds, Shuttle No. 2, 1 ds, j to last p of sr. 3 ds, cl.

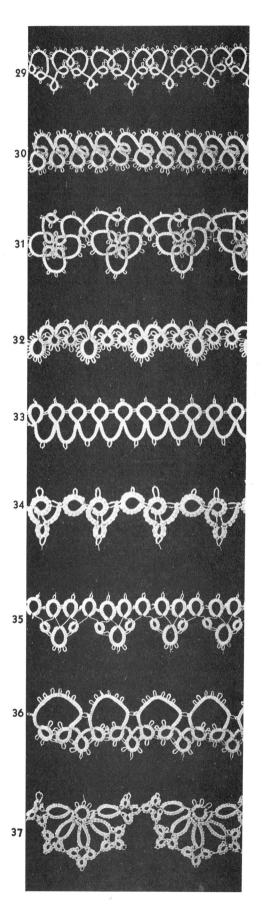

Continued from Page 23

site r. 4 ds, cl, ch 6 ds, r 4 ds, j to p of opposite r, 5 ds, p, 4 ds, cl, ch 6 ds, r 4 ds, p, 5 ds, p, 4 ds, cl, ch 6 ds, j to p of opposite ch, 6 ds, p. 6 ds, r 4 ds, j to p of last r, 5 ds, p, 4 ds, cl, ch 10 ds, p, 10 ds, r 4 ds, j to p of last r, 5 ds, p, 4 ds, cl, ch 6 ds, p, 6 ds, p, 6 ds, r 4 ds, j to p of last r, 5 ds, j to p of opposite r, 4 ds, cl, ch 6 ds, r 4 ds, j to p of opposite r. 5 ds, p, 4 ds, cl, ch 6 ds, r 4 ds, p, 5 ds, p, 4 ds, cl, ch 6 ds, j to p of opposite ch. 6 ds, p, 6 ds, r 4 ds, j to p of last r. 5 ds, p. 4 ds. cl, ch 6 ds, p, 6 ds, p, 6 ds, r 4 ds, j to p of last r, 5 ds, p, 4 ds, cl, ch 6 ds, p. 6 ds, p, 6 ds. r 4 ds, j to p of last r, 5 ds. j to p of opposite r, 4 ds. cl. ch 6 ds, r 4 ds, j to p of opposite r. 5 ds. j to p of opposite r, 4 ds, cl, ch 6 ds. r 4 ds, j to p of opposite r, 5 ds, p, 4 ds, cl, ch 6 ds, j to p of opposite ch, 6 ds, p, 6 ds, r 4 ds, j to p of last r, 5 ds, j to p of opposite r, 4 ds, cl, ch 6 ds. r 4 ds, j to p of opposite r, 5 ds, p, 4 ds, cl, ch 6 ds, r 4 ds, p, 5 ds, p, 4 ds, cl, ch 6 ds, j to p of opposite ch, 6 ds, p, 6 ds, r 4 ds, j to p of last r, 5 ds, p, 4 ds, cl, ch 6 ds, r 4 ds, p, 5 ds, p, 4 ds, cl, ch 6 ds, r 4 ds, p, 5 ds, p, 4 ds, cl, ch 6 ds, j to p of opposite ch, 6 ds, j to p of opposite ch, 6 ds, r 4 ds, j to p of last r, 5 ds, p, 4 ds, cl, ch 6 ds, j to p of opposite ch, 6 ds, p, 6 ds, r 4 ds, j to p of last r, 5 ds, p, 4 ds, cl, ch 6 ds, p, 6 ds, p, 6 ds, r 4 ds. j to p of last r, 5 ds, j to p of opposite r, 4 ds, cl, ch 6 ds, r 4 ds, j to p of opposite r, 5 ds, p, 4 ds, cl, ch 6 ds, r 4 ds, p, 5 ds, p, 4 ds, cl, ch 6 ds, j to p of opposite ch, 6 ds, p, 6 ds, r 4 ds, j to p of last r, 5 ds, p, 4 ds, cl, ch 6 ds, r 4 ds. p. 5 ds. p. 4 ds. cl, ch 6 ds, p, 6 ds, p, 6 ds, r 4 ds, j to p of last r. 5 ds. p. 4 ds, cl, ch 6 ds. Repeat from * for each point. **Make small medallion between points as follows:** R 4 ds, j to p of center ch between points, 5 ds, p, 4 ds. cl. ch 6 ds, j to p of opposite ch, 6 ds, p, 6 ds, r 4 ds. j to p of last r, 5 ds, p, 4 ds, cl, ch 6 ds, p, 6 ds. p. 6 ds, r 4 ds, j to p of last r, 5 ds, p. 4 ds, cl, ch 6 ds. p. 6 ds, j to p of ch on next point, 6 ds, r 4 ds, j to p of ch between the 2 points, 5 ds, j to p of last r, 4 ds, cl. Tie and cut.

SCALLOP EDGING No. 18
(2 Shuttles)

Heading: R 5 ds, 3 p sep by 5 ds, 5 ds, cl, turn, ch 4 ds, r 5 ds, 3 p sep by 5 ds, 5 ds, cl, * turn, ch 4 ds, r 5 ds, j to third p of first r, 5 ds, p, 5 ds, p, 5 ds, cl, turn, ch 4 ds, r 5 ds, j to p of opposite r, 5 ds, p, 5 ds, p, 5 ds, cl. Repeat r and ch for desired length. **Scallops:** *Lr 4 ds, j to middle p of first r of heading, 4 ds, p, 4 ds, p. 4 ds, cl, turn, ch 4 ds, sr 3 ds, j to p of next r of heading, 3 ds, p, 3 ds, p, 3 ds, cl, turn, ch 4 ds, lr 4 ds, j to first p of first lr, 4 ds, p, 4 ds, p, 4 ds, cl, turn,

ch 4 ds, sr 3 ds, j to third p of first sr, 3 ds, p, 3 ds, p, 3 ds, cl, turn. Repeat, alternating large and small r with ch between until there are 21 lr and 20 sr, each j to preceding r, j last p of sr and lr to eleventh and twelfth r of heading. Repeat from * for each scallop, j middle p of first lr to p of last lr of preceding scallop. **Center Ring:** *10 lp sep by 3 ds, cl, tie and cut thread. R 6 ds, j to lp of center r, 6 ds, cl, ch 5 ds, p, 5 ds, j to third free r of heading, 5 ds, p, 5 ds, r 6 ds, j to next lp of lr, 6 ds, cl, turn; ch 5 ds, 3 p sep by 5 ds, 5 ds, repeat until there are 10 sr and 9 ch, j center p of fourth and fifth ch to tenth and eleventh sr of scallop and middle p of last ch to sixth free r of heading. Cut and tie thread. Repeat from * for each scallop.

WIDE EDGE No. 19
(2 Shuttles)

1st row: * R 5 ds, 3 p sep by 5 ds, 5 ds, cl, ch 7 ds, p, 7 ds. Repeat from * for desired length, j first p of each r to the last p of preceding r.

2nd row: R 5 ds, 3 p sep by 5 ds, 5 ds, cl, ch 10 ds, j to p of ch of first row, 10 ds, * r 5 ds, 3 p sep by 5 ds, 5 ds, cl, ch 10 ds, sk 1 ch of last r, j to p of next ch, 10 ds. Repeat from * across.

3rd row: R 5 ds, j to last p of first r of second row, 5 ds, p, 5 ds, j to p of next r of second row, 5 ds, cl, ch 10 ds, p, 10 ds. Repeat the r and ch across, j as directed.

4th row: Lr 6 ds, p. 6 ds, j to p of ch of last row, 6 ds, p, 6 ds, cl, * turn, sp, sr 6 ds, lp, 6 ds, cl, turn, sp, lr 6 ds, j to third p of last lr, 6 ds, 2 p sep by 6 ds, 6 ds, cl, turn, sp, sr 6 ds, j to lp of last sr, 6 ds, cl, turn, sp, lr 6 ds, j to third p of last lr, 6 ds, j to p of next ch of last row, 6 ds. p, 6 ds, cl. Repeat from * across.

5th row: Lr 6 ds, 3 p sep by 6 ds, 6 ds, cl, turn, sp, sr 6 ds, j to lp of last row, 6 ds, cl. * turn, sp, lr 6 ds, j to third p of last lr, 6 ds, 2 p sep by 6 ds, 6 ds, cl, turn, sp, sr 6 ds, j to same lp of last row, 6 ds, cl, turn, sp, lr 6 ds, j to third p of last lr, 6 ds, 2 p sep by 6 ds, 6 ds, cl, turn, sp, sr 6 ds, j to next lp of last row, 6 ds, cl. Repeat from * across.

6th row: R 6 ds, 3 p sep by 6 ds. 6 ds, cl, ch 11 ds, j to p of first lr of last row, 11 ds, * r 6 ds, p, 6 ds, j to second p of last r, 6 ds, p, 6 ds, cl, r 6 ds, j to last p of last r, 4 ds, 5 p sep by 2 ds, 4 ds, p, 6 ds, cl, r 6 ds, j to last p of last r, 6 ds, 2 p sep by 6 ds, 6 ds, cl, ch 11 ds, sk 1 r of last row, j to p of next r of last row, 11 ds. Repeat from * across.

Continued from Page 24

ds, cl, (ch 6 ds, r 3 ds, 3 p sep by 2 ds, 3 ds, cl) twice, ch 6 ds, j in p of opposite ch. 6 ds, p. 6 ds, r 3 ds, p, 2 ds, j in center p of last r, 2 ds, p, 3 ds, cl. (ch 6 ds, r 3 ds, 3 p sep by 2 ds, 3 ds, cl) twice, ch 6 ds, j in p of opposite ch. 6 ds, j in p of next opposite ch, 6 ds, r 3 ds. j in third p of last r. 2 ds, p, 2 ds, p, 3 ds, cl. turn, ch 6 ds, j in p of opposite ch. 6 ds, p, 2 ds, p, 6 ds, turn, r 3 ds, j in third p of last r. 2 ds, p, 2 ds, p, 3 ds, cl, ch 6 ds, p, 2 ds, p, 6 ds, p, 6 ds, r 3 ds j in p of last r, 2 ds, p. 2 ds, j in first p of first r of group. 3 ds, cl. ch 6 ds.

turn, r 3 ds, j in third p of opposite r, 2 ds, p, 2 ds, p, 3 ds, cl, ch 6 ds, turn, r 3 ds, 3 p sep by 2 ds, 3 ds, cl, ch 6 ds, j in p of opposite ch. 6 ds, p, 2 ds, p, 6 ds, turn, r 3 ds, j in third p of last r, 2 ds, p, 2 ds, p, 3 ds, cl, turn, ch 6 ds, p, 2 ds, p, 6 ds, p, 6 ds, turn. r 3 ds, j in third p of last r, 2 ds, p, 2 ds, p, 3 ds, cl, turn, (ch 6 ds, p) twice. 6 ds, r 3 ds, j in third p of last r, 2 ds, p, 2 ds, j in first p of first r of group, 3 ds, cl, turn, ch 6 ds, turn. r 3 ds, j in third p of opposite r, 2 ds, p. 2 ds, p, 3 ds, cl, turn, ch 6 ds, turn. r 3 ds, 3 p sep by 2 ds, 3 ds, cl. Repeat from *.

OVAL DOILY SET
Continued from Page 11

6 ds, 5 p sep by 2 ds, 6 ds, sr 6 ds, j to last p of lr, 6 ds, cl, sr 6 ds, p, 6 ds, cl, ch 6 ds, 5 p sep by 2 ds, 6 ds, lr 5 ds, j to p of sr, 2 ds, 10 p sep by 2 ds, 5 ds, cl, ch 6 ds, 5 p sep by 2 ds, 6 ds, sr 6 ds, j to last p of lr, 6 ds, cl, sr 6 ds, p, 6 ds, cl, ch 6 ds, 5 p sep by 2 ds, 6 ds, lr 5 ds, j to p of sr, 2 ds, 4 p sep by 2 ds, 2 ds, j to center p of next ch, 2 ds, 5 p sep by 2 ds, 5 ds, cl, ch 6 ds, 5 p sep by 2 ds, 6 ds. Repeat r and ch across short rows between the medallions and around end medallion.

2nd row: R 3 ds, 3 p sep by 3 ds, 3 ds, cl, ch 6 ds, r 3 ds, 3 p sep by 3 ds, 3 ds, cl, ch 6 ds, r 3 ds, j to last p of first r, 3 ds, j to center p of ch of last row, 3 ds, p, 3 ds, cl, * ch 6 ds, r 3 ds, j to last p of opposite r, 3 ds, 2 p sep by 3 ds, 3 ds, cl, ch 6 ds, r 3 ds, j to last p of opposite r, 3 ds, 2 p sep by 3 ds, 3 ds, cl, ch 6 ds, r 3 ds, j to p of opposite r, 3 ds, 2 p sep by 3 ds, 3 ds, cl, ch 6 ds, r 3 ds, j to p of opposite r, 3 ds, j to center

p of next ch of last row, 3 ds, p, 3 ds, cl. Repeat from * around. Tie and cut.

3rd row: Make like third row of medallion, j center p of ch to p of r of last row, sk 3 r of second row between each ch at lower edge.

4th row: Sr 6 ds, p, 6 ds, cl, * lr 5 ds, 4 p sep by 5 ds, 5 ds, cl, ch 5 ds, 3 p sep by 5 ds, 5 ds, sr 6 ds, j to second p of lr, 6 ds, cl, lr 5 ds, p, 5 ds, j to center p of ch of last row, 5 ds, 2 p sep by 5 ds, 5 ds, cl, ch 5 ds, 3 p sep by 5 ds, 5 ds, sr 6 ds, j to second p of last lr, 6 ds, cl. Repeat from * around. Tie and cut.

5th row: Repeat third row of medallion, j by center p of ch, as in illustration.

SMALL DOILY

Make a medallion as for oval doily Make the fourth row of this like the third row of the directions, j the points of the flowers together, as in illustration.

RECTANGULAR LUNCHEON SET
Continued from Page 18

ch 5 ds, p, 2 ds, j to center p of next r of last row, 2 ds, p, 5 ds. Repeat from * around, working each corner same as first corner. Tie and cut.

8th row: Repeat the fifth row, omitting the four r in corners and making a ch same as the other ch. Tie and cut.

9th row: Make small motifs like center motifs. Join to last row by j center p of first r to third p of ch, and center p of next r to first p of next ch. Join motifs together same as for center. Tie and cut.

10th row: Make another row of motifs. Join as in center.

11th row: * R 5 ds, j to third p of r of motif, 5 ds, j to first p of next r of same motif, 5 ds, cl, turn, ch 3 ds, 9 p

sep by 2 ds, 3 ds, turn. Repeat from * around, making 12 p in the ch at each corner instead of 9 p.

FOR MEDIUM-SIZE DOILY

Make the center, first, second, third, fourth, fifth, ninth and eleventh rows like large doily.

FOR SMALL RECTANGULAR DOILY

Make the center and first, second and third rows as in large doily.

FOR SMALL SQUARE DOILY

Make 2 rows of motifs with 2 motifs each. Make first, second and third rows as in large doily.

Luncheon Set—Medallion Shamrock Edge

(On Four Corners of Page 32)

ROUND DOILY

(Use 2 Shuttles, and No. 30 Crochet Cotton)

Center: R 12 p sep by 2 ds, cl. Tie and cut.

1st row: Lr 4 ds, 7 p, 4 ds, cl, * turn. sp (⅛ inch), sr 4 ds. j to p of center, 4 ds, cl, turn, sp, lr 4 ds, j to seventh p of last lr, 6 p, d 4s, cl. Repeat from * around. Tie and cut.

2d row: Lr 4 ds, 9 p, 4 ds, cl, * turn. sp, sr 3 ds, p. 3 ds, j to third p of lr (last row), 3 ds, p, 3 ds, cl, turn, sp. lr 4 ds, j to ninth p of last lr, 8 p, 4 ds. cl, turn, sp, sr 3 ds. j to third p of sr, 3 ds, sk 1 p, j to next p of same lr, 3 ds. p. 3 ds, cl, turn sp, lr 4 ds, j to ninth p of lr, 8 p, 4 ds, cl. Repeat from * around. Tie and cut.

3d row: Join thread to center p of r, * ch 9 ds, p, 9 ds, j to center p of next r. Repeat from * around. Tie and cut.

4th row: Lr 4 ds, 9 p, 4 ds, cl, turn, sp, sr 4 ds, p, 4 ds, j to p of ch (last row), 4 ds, p, 4 ds, cl, * turn, sp, r 4 ds, j to ninth p of last lr, 4 ds, 2 p sep by 4 ds, 4 ds, cl. turn, sp, sr 4 ds, j to third p of last sr, 4 ds, 2 p sep by 4 ds, 4 ds, cl, * turn, sp, lr 4 ds, j to third p of r, 8 p, 4 ds, cl, turn, sp. sr 4 ds, j to third p of last sr, 4 ds, j to p of next ch, 4 ds, p, 4 ds, cl. Repeat from * around. Tie and cut.

5th row: R 4 ds, 7 p sep by 2 ds, 4 ds, cl, (r 4 ds, j to seventh p of last r, 6 p sep by 2 ds, 4 ds, cl) twice, r 4 ds, j to seventh p of last r, 2 p sep by 2 ds, 2 ds, j to center p of lr (last row), 2 ds, 2 p sep by 2 ds, 2 ds, j to first p of first r, 4 ds, cl. Repeat the motif all around, j each together and to lr of last row by center p.

6th row: Sr 4 ds, 5 p, 4 ds, cl, * turn, ch 4 ds, 5 p sep by 2 ds, 4 ds, turn, r 4 ds, 3 p. 2 ds, j to fifth p of last r, 2 ds, 3 p, 4 ds, cl, r 4 ds, 3 p, 2 ds, j to center p of r of motif. 2 ds, 3 p. 4 ds, cl, r 4 ds, 7 p, 4 ds, cl, turn, ch 4 ds, 5 p. 4ds, turn, sr 4 ds, j to center p of last r, 4 p, 4 ds, cl. Repeat from * around. Tie and cut.

7th row: * R 4 ds, 7 p sep by 2 ds, 4 ds, cl, turn, ch 3 ds, 3 p sep by 2 ds, 3 ds, turn, r 4 ds, 3 p sep by 2 ds, 2 ds, j to center p of ch of last row, 2 ds, 3 p sep by 2 ds. 4 ds, cl, turn, ch 3 ds, 3 p sep by 2 ds, 3 ds, turn. Repeat from * around. Tie and cut.

8th row: * R 4 ds, 7 p sep by 2 ds, 4 ds, cl, turn, ch 4 ds, 2 p sep by 3 ds, 3 ds, j to center p of r (last row), 3 ds, 2 p sep by 3 ds, 4 ds, turn. Repeat from * around. Tie and cut.

9th row: Join thread in center p of r of last row, * ch 2 ds, 7 p, 2 ds, j in center p of next r of last row. Repeat from * around. Tie and cut.

MEDALLIONS FOR EDGE

Center: R 4 ds, 7 p, 4 ds, cl, (r 4 ds, j to seventh p of last r, 6 p, 4 ds, cl) 4 times, j the last r to first r. Tie and cut.

Edge: (R 4 ds, 7 p, 4 ds, cl) 3 times, * turn, ch 5 ds, 2 p sep by 2 ds, 2 ds, j to center p of r (center), 2 ds, 2 p sep by 2 ds, 5 ds, turn, r 4 ds, 3 p, j to center p of last r, 3 p, 4 ds, cl, (r 4 ds, 7 p, 4 ds, cl) twice. Repeat from * one more time, turn, (ch 5 ds, 2 p sep by 2 ds, 2 ds. Join to center p of next center r, 2 ds, 2 p sep by 2 ds, 5 ds, turn, r 4 ds, 3 p, j to center p of last r, 3 p, 4 ds, cl, r 4 ds, 3 p, j to center p of ch (last row), 3 p, 4 ds, cl, r 4 ds, 7 p. 4 ds, cl) twice, ch 5 ds, 2 p sep by 2 ds. 2 ds. j to fourth p of next center r, 2 ds, 2 p sep by 2 ds, 5 ds, turn, r 4 ds, 3 p, j to center p of last r, 3 p, 4 ds, cl, r 4 ds, 7 p, 4 ds, cl, r 4 ds, 3 p, j to center p of first r, 3 p, 4 ds, cl, turn, ch 5 ds, 2 p sep by 2 ds, 2 ds, j to next p of same r with last ch, 2 ds, 2 p sep by 2 ds, 5 ds, j to first group of three r. Tie and cut.

SMALL DOILY

Center: R 14 p sep by 2 ds, cl. Tie and cut.
Make first and second rows of large doily. Then make medallions for edge as directed above.

To Join Medallions: Join center p of center r of shamrock to center p of r of last row. Skip 1 r of last row between each shamrock of the medallions.

MEDIUM SIZE DOILY

To make a doily in medium size for a luncheon set, repeat the directions for the large round doily through the eighth row.

DIRECTIONS—MEDALLIONS

Continued from Page 20

1st row: *R 10 ds, j to center p of r of motif, 10 ds, cl, ch 5 ds, 3 p sep by 3 ds, 5 ds, r 10 ds, j to same p with last r, 10 ds, cl, ch 5 ds, 3 p sep by 3 ds, 5 ds. Repeat from * around. Tie and cut.

2d row: *R 10 ds, p, 10 ds, cl, r 10 ds, j to center p of ch of last row, 10 ds, cl, r 10 ds, p, 10 ds, cl, (ch 3 ds, sr 4 ds, p. 4 ds, cl) twice, ch 9 ds, p, 9 ds, (sr 4 ds, p, 4 ds, cl, ch 3 ds) twice, r 10 ds, j to p of opposite r, 10 ds, cl, r 10 ds, j to first p of next ch, 10 ds, cl, r 10 ds, p, 10 ds, cl, (ch 3 ds, r 4 ds, j to p of opposite sr, 4 ds, cl) twice, ch 9 ds, p, 9 ds, (sr 4 ds, p, 4 ds, cl, ch 3 ds) twice, r 10 ds, j to p of opposite r, 10 ds, cl, r 10 ds, j to third p of same ch, 10 ds, cl, 10 ds, p, 10 ds, cl, (ch 3 ds, r 4 ds, j to p of opposite sr, 4 ds, cl) twice, ch 9 ds, p, 9 ds, (sr 4 ds, p, 4 ds, cl, ch 3 ds) twice. Repeat from * around, j r as shown. Tie and cut.

MEDALLION (3d Column, Bottom)
(2 Shuttles)

1st row: R 10 ds, lp, 10 ds, cl, (ch 5 ds, 5 p sep by 2 ds. 5 ds, r 10 ds, j to lp of first r, 10 ds, cl) 3 times, ch 5 ds, 5 p sep by 2 ds, 5 ds. Tie and cut.

2d row: *R 10 ds, j to center p of ch of last row, 10 ds, cl. ch 7 ds, 5 p sep by 2 ds, 7 ds, r 10 ds, p, 10 ds, cl, ch 7 ds. 5 p sep by 2 ds, 7 ds. Repeat from * around. Tie and cut.

3d row: R 10 ds, lp, 10 ds, cl, (ch 7 ds, 5 p sep by 2 ds. 7 ds, r 10 ds, j to lp of first r, 10 ds, cl) 3 times, * ch 7 ds. 2 p sep by 2 ds, 2 ds, j to center p of ch of last row, 2 ds, 2 p sep by 2 ds, 7 ds, r 10 ds, lp, 10 ds, cl, ch 7 ds, p, 2 ds, j to fourth p of opposite ch, 2 ds, 3 p sep by 2 ds, 7 ds. (r 10 ds, j to lp of first r, 10 ds, cl, ch 7 ds, 5 p sep by 2 ds, 7 ds) twice, r 10 ds, j to lp of first r, 10 ds, cl. Repeat from * around. Tie and cut.

LUNCHEON SET

Continued from Page 19

ch 4 ds, turn, lr 5 ds, 7 p sep by 2 ds, 5 ds, cl, lr 5 ds, j to seventh p of last lr, 2 ds, 2 p sep by 2 ds, 2 ds, j to center p of lr of last row, 2 ds, 3 p sep by 2 ds, 5 ds, cl, lr 5 ds, j to seventh p of last lr, 2 ds, 6 p sep by 2 ds, 5 ds, cl, turn, ch 4 ds, turn, sr 3 ds, 3 p sep by 3 ds, 3 ds, cl, turn, ch 4 ds, turn, sr 3 ds, j to third p of sr, 3 ds, 2 p sep by 3 ds, 3 ds, cl, j at base of opposite sr, turn, ch 5 ds, 7 p sep by 2 ds, 5 ds, turn, lr 5 ds, 2 p sep by 2 ds, 2 ds, j to center p of sr, 2 ds, j to center p of next sr, 2 ds, 3 p sep by 2 ds, 5 ds, cl, (lr 5 ds, j to seventh p of last lr, 2 ds, 6 p sep by 2 ds, 5 ds, cl) twice. Repeat from * around. Tie and cut.

3rd row: Make 6 medallions, using directions for center and first row. Join fourth p of center r of 2 clusters (3 lr) to center p of 2 ch of last row and sk 1 ch between each medallion.

4th row: R 6 ds, j to center p of ch between 2 medallions, 6 ds, cl, turn, ch 9 ds, turn, (r 6 ds, j to p between the 2 clusters of 3 lr of medallion, 6 ds, cl, turn, ch 5 ds, 5 p sep by 2 ds, 5 ds, turn, r 6 ds, j to center p of center r of cluster, 6 ds, cl, turn, ch 5 ds, 5 p sep by 2 ds, 5 ds, turn) 8 times, r 6 ds, j between 2 clusters, 6 ds, cl, turn, ch 9 ds, turn, r 6 ds, j to center p of ch between 2 medallions, 6 ds, cl, turn, ch 9 ds, turn, r 6 ds, j to p between the 2 clusters of 3 lr of next medallion, 6 ds, cl, turn, ch 5 ds, 2 p sep by 2 ds, 2 ds, j to center p of opposite ch, 2 ds, 2 p sep by 2 ds, 5 ds. Repeat around each medallion. Tie and cut.

5th row: * R 6 ds, j to center p of ch (to left) between 2 scallops, 3 ds, j to center p of opposite ch (to right), 6 ds, cl, turn, ch 8 ds, turn, (r 6 ds, j to center p of next ch, 6 ds, cl, turn, ch 5 ds, 5 p sep by 2 ds, 5 ds, turn)

twice, (r 6 ds, j to second p of next ch, 6 ds, cl, turn, ch 5 ds, 5 p sep by 2 ds, 5 ds, turn, r 6 ds, j to fourth p of same ch, 6 ds, cl, turn, ch 5 ds, 5 p sep by 2 ds, 5 ds, turn, r 6 ds, j to center p of next ch, 6 ds, cl, turn, ch 5 ds, 5 p sep by 2 ds, 5 ds, turn) 5 times, ch 8 ds, turn. Repeat from * around. Tie and cut.

6th row: Make like fifth row, j r to center p of each ch of last row. Tie and cut.

7th row: Make like sixth row, having 7 p in ch instead of 5 p.

8th row: Make like first row, sk the 2 ch at base of scallop, j the sr to third and fifth p of ch of last row.

9th row: * R 6 ds, j to center p of lr between 2 scallops, 6 ds, cl, (turn, ch 4 ds, 7 p sep by 2 ds, 4 ds, turn, r 6 ds, j to center p of next center r of cluster, 6 ds, cl, turn, ch 4 ds, 7 p sep by 2 ds, 4 ds, turn, r 6 ds, j to p between 2 clusters, 6 ds, cl) 10 times, (turn, ch 4 ds, 7 p sep by 2 ds, 4 ds, turn, r 6 ds, j to center p of lr, 6 ds, cl) 3 times, turn, ch 4 ds, 7 p sep by 2 ds, 4 ds, turn. Repeat from * around. Tie and cut.

FOR MEDIUM-SIZE DOILY

Make center as for large doily and omit sixth and seventh rows of large doily, and add eighth and ninth rows.

FOR SMALL DOILY

Make 6 medallions as in large doily. Join 5 around 1 medallion by center p of 2 center r of clusters. Then make a row around the medallions like outer row of large doily.

LARGE ROUND DOILY

Continued from Page 6

8th row: * R 5 ds, 3 p sep by 5 ds, 5 ds, cl, (ch 10 ds, j to fourth p of a scallop of last row, 10 ds), r 5 ds, 3 p sep by 5 ds, 5 ds, cl, ch 10 ds, sk 2 p of same scallop, j in next p, 10 ds, repeat from * around, j. Tie and cut.

9th row: * R 5 ds, j to third p of a r, 5 ds, p, 5 ds, j to first p of next r, 5 ds, cl, ch 2 ds, 9 p sep by 2 ds, 2 ds, repeat from * around. Tie and cut.

10th row: Tie the 2 shuttle threads together, lr 1 ds, p, 3 ds, j to center p of scallop, 3 ds, 2 p sep by 3 ds, 3 ds, r st 2 ds, p, 3 ds, (sep r 2 ds, p, 2 ds, cl) 3 times, sp ¼ inch (sr, 2 ds, p, 2 ds, cl) 3 times, (3 ds, 2 p sep by 3 ds, 3 ds) on unfinished r, cl, * tie both threads together close to lr, shuttle No. 1, (sr 2 ds, p 2 ds) 3 times, with shuttle No. 2 make 3 sr like cluster just made. Tie both threads together close to last sr, lr 3 ds, 5 p sep by 3 ds, 3 ds, r st 3 ds, p, 3 ds, cl. Tie threads close to lr. Make another group of 3 sr like others, lr 3 ds, 2 p sep by 3 ds, 3 ds, sk 1 scallop, j to center p of next scallop, 3 ds, 2 p sep by 3 ds, 3 ds, r st 3 ds, 2 p sep by 3 ds, 3 ds, cl, repeat from * around ending with lr (3 ds, p, 3 ds, j in center of sp of first group of sr, 3 ds, 2 p sep by 3 ds, 3 ds, r st 3 ds, 2 p sep by 3 ds, 3 ds, cl. Tie and cut.

11th row: * R 5 ds, 3 p sep by 5 ds, 5 ds, cl, ch 2 ds, 4 p sep by 2 ds, 2 ds, j to center p of lr, 2 ds, 4 p sep

by 2 ds, 2 ds, (r 5 ds, 3 p sep by 5 ds, 5 ds, cl, ch 2 ds, 9 p sep by 2 ds, 2 ds) twice, repeat from * around. Tie and cut.

Make 15 medallions using the first 4 rows of the doily. Join the medallions together by center p of 3 scallops, (for first 2 medallions), sk 8 scallops, j third medallion to center p of next 3 scallops, j all together making a circle.

12th row: R 5 ds, j to third p of a r, 5 ds, p, 5 ds, j to first p of next r, 5 ds, cl, ch 2 ds, 9 p sep by 2 ds, 2 ds, r 5 ds, j to third p of last r, 5 ds, p, 5 ds, j to first p of next r, 5 ds, cl, ch 2 ds, 4 p sep by 2 ds, (counting from left of medallion) sk 1 scallop, j to center p of next medallion scallop, 2 ds, 4 p sep by 2 ds, 2 ds, r 5 ds, j to third p of last r, 5 ds, p, 5 ds, j to first p of next r, 5 ds, cl, ch 2 ds, 2 p sep by 2 ds, 2 ds, j to center p of next scallop of medallion, 2 ds, 3 p sep by 2 ds, 2 ds, j to center p of next scallop, 2 ds, 2 p sep by 2 ds, 2 ds, r 5 ds, j to third p of last r, 5 ds, p, 5 ds, j to first p of next r, 5 ds, cl, ch 2 ds, 4 p sep by 2 ds, 2 ds, j to center p of next scallop of medallion, 2 ds, 4 p sep by 2 ds, 2 ds, repeat from * around. Tie and cut.

TUMBLER DOILY TO MATCH

Make the center and first 9 rows of above doily.

Helpful Suggestions

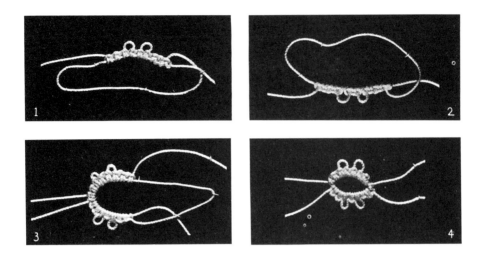

DIRECTIONS FOR THE REVERSE STITCH

Begin ring, making three double stitches, picot, two double stitches, picot, three double stitches (figure one) (this is one-half of ring), take work off from hand* (reverse), turn over (figure two), put work on hand so that the thread which was under is now over the hand. Take shuttle No. 2 and make the other half of the ring, with the reverse stitch, which is done by holding the thread on the hand taut, and making the stitch with the thread from the shuttle, making three double stitches, picot, two double stitches, picot, three double stitches (figure three), take work from hand, turn over*, take shuttle No. 1 and close ring (figure four).

In joining while doing reverse work, do not draw shuttle very taut after passing through joining loop, but draw the loop back again so that the joining stitch is made with the thread from shuttle and the thread on the hand may be drawn back and forth.

AN OLD ART REVIVED

Let's all start tatting together! When one sees the effective new designs shown here and the lovely thread on the market, the discriminating needleworker will be intrigued by the possibilities of the combination, which are endless, and will not rest until the work takes form under her hands and is completed.

There will be found lovely colors as well as white in both crochet and tatting cotton and there also comes another type that is called "shaded," the colors being pink, blue, yellow, lavender, green, and black and white, in toning of the same color, which makes ideal trimmings for dainty handkerchiefs. There is also made a range of tinted colors in this tatting cotton—that is, combinations of different colors with white that are well balanced both in hue and tone. One will love the articles that are made with them.

However, after seeing the specialized materials available today, one will wonder how needleworkers of olden times made such beautiful lasting articles from the threads then obtainable. The thread used was coarser, rougher, and with no regularity of spinning, for tatting is an old lace-making art and has come down to us from the Middle Ages, when it apparently developed in several parts of the world.

The Italians gave it a name meaning "eye," because of the similarity of the rings to the eyes; the French gave it a name to describe its delicate appearance; the Orientals call it by a word meaning "the shuttle," which is used in making; and in America, it is called "tatting," probably from the word "tatters," as it is made in sections which are then connected.

Designs in the early days, before the printing press was invented, were handed from neighbor to neighbor and copied in this way; but today, the large modern illustrations and clear directions make the work very easy. It is suggested that the directions, abbreviations, and notes be carefully read before starting work.

There is included in this book the most useful up-to-date articles for this work, from tiny edgings of the finest thread for handkerchiefs, dainty baby caps, a lacy yoke for silk underwear, to medallions and edgings with which to decorate linens; also doilies of several sizes, and a chair set for medium-size threads. Many of these lovely articles may be made of different size thread, depending on the space in which they are to be used. As coarse a thread as size No. 10 is practical if desired.

There is really no limit to the possibilities of tatting, for this needle-art is composed of knots and stitches, made lacy with loops of picots, for the different arrangements produce many and varied patterns, as shown in the preceding pages.

Tatting is a form of lace made with a tatting shuttle, and for some designs only one shuttle is needed, while for others two are required. In the latter case, it is more convenient to have a second shuttle.

Instructions for Tatting

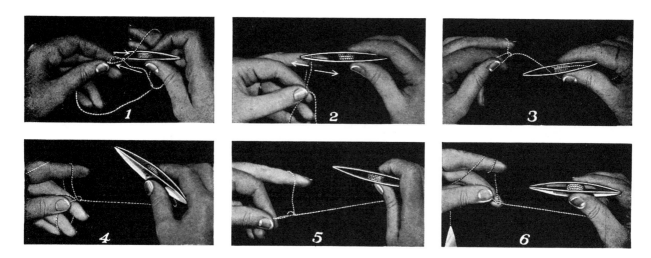

As will be judged, the simplest form of tatting is the ring which is made with one shuttle, and when a chain is introduced, the second shuttle is required. In learning to tat, the knot is made on the shuttle thread, and not with it though all the action is taken with the shuttle thread, shown in illustration No. 3. A second important fact to remember is that the shuttle thread is pulled taut before the knot is tightened.

First, wind the thread around the bobbin in the shuttle, layer over layer, but the thread should never extend over the edge.

To make a ring: Hold the shuttle between the thumb and forefinger of the right hand as shown. Hold the end of the thread between the thumb and forefinger of the left hand and pass it around the fingers of this hand, not too tightly, crossing it under the thumb. It is with this loop of thread that the ring is worked and this is called the ring thread. Throw the shuttle thread over the right hand as in illustration No. 1. Pass the shuttle between the first and second fingers of left hand under the shuttle and ring threads and back over ring thread, allowing the ring thread to fall slack by bringing the four fingers of the left hand together. Pull shuttle thread taut, then open the fingers of the left hand until the loop is caught with the thumb, as shown in No. 3.

For the second half, the thread is dropped instead of raised, shuttle is passed over the left-hand thread instead of under (as before), is brought through below, between the two threads (as before) and drawn up in the same way. (Illustration No. 2.) Illustration No. 4 shows the second half of stitch slipping into place beside the first half.

This group is called a double stitch and is the main stitch used in tatting. In making this, it will be found that by pulling the shuttle thread and then the ring thread, the stitch slips back and forth on the shuttle thread. If it does not, the stitch has been locked and must be made over again.

Illustration No. 5 shows a picot which is made by leaving a space of thread between the stitches, and to join two picots, draw the working thread through the picot and pass shuttle through loop. Then draw up close to resemble a half stitch, but not to be counted as one.

Two shuttles are required to make a design having a chain. Tie the threads together and hold between the thumb and second finger of the left hand and with the first finger outstretched, wind the thread around it two or three times, allowing the second shuttle to drop as on No. 6. The stitches for the chain are made with the thread between the first and second fingers in the same way as those for the rings.

ABBREVIATIONS IN TATTING

r st—reverse stitch.	p—picot.	j—join, joined, joining.	lr—large ring.
sl st—slip stitch.	ch—chain.	sp—space.	sr—small ring.
ds—double stitch.	s ch—short chain.	cl—close.	lp ch—long picot chain.
r—ring.	l ch—long chain.	sep—separated.	sk—skip.
	lp—long picot.	p ch—picot chain.	

NOTES

All beginners should use coarse thread to see work better.

Never break off thread after winding shuttle if directions call for chain (ch). When a shuttle has a point or hook, be careful to keep point forward. Rings are to be made close together unless directions call for space (sp). A ring is always to be drawn close unless otherwise stated. Space means to allow thread between last ring and new one. When making medallions, doilies, or centerpieces, the work will be lovelier and easier to do if it is pressed every two or three rows, in the desired form, and to do this place on a thick pad, shape, and press over a damp cloth, and then a dry one, until the piece is dry. This will show how the work is going, and will keep it from being too full or too tight.